Shabbat: The Right Way

Resolving Halachic Dilemmas

SHABBAT: THE RIGHT WAY

RESOLVING HALACHIC DILEMMAS

RABBI J. SIMCHA COHEN

URIM PUBLICATIONS

Jerusalem • New York

With appreciation to the Epstein and Langfan families.

Shabbat: The Right Way: Resolving Halachic Dilemmas
By Rabbi J. Simcha Cohen
Copyright © 2009 by Rabbi J. Simcha Cohen

Printed in Israel. First Edition.
ISBN-13: 978-965-524-021-4
Urim Publications
P.O. Box 52287, Jerusalem 91521 Israel

Lambda Publishers Inc.
527 Empire Blvd., Brooklyn, New York 11225 U.S.A.
Tel: 718-972-5449 Fax: 718-972-6307, mh@ejudaica.com

www.UrimPublications.com

Dedicated by the Rechnitz Family
Los Angeles, California

In memory of

HENRY RECHNITZ ז"ל
R' YITZCHOK ZVI BEN SHLOMO

נפטר ז' תמוז תשס"ח

IN MEMORIAM

I have known Henry Rechnitz ז"ל for many years.
He was an extremely fine and noble person:
a consummate gentleman, always courtly, gentle and cordial.
He went out of his way to make all feel welcome in his presence.
Love, care and devotion to family served as a guiding principle of his lifestyle.
No matter the need, he was there to respond.
Kavod HaTorah and Kavod HaRabonut were not just lofty goals, but, rather,
integral parts of his moral character that were taught to his children.
His devoted wife, children, grandchildren, and great grandchildren,
together with Klal Yisrael,
have lost a true family patriarch.

יהי זכרו ברוך

Rabbi J. Simcha Cohen

מַעֲשֵׂה אָבוֹת סִימָן לְבָנִים

This Sefer is dedicated
In loving memory of
Our Dad and Mom

MICHAEL & DORA ETHEL PARISER ע"ה

By the Paul S. Pariser Foundation
Big Sky, Montana

With gratitude and appreciation to HaShem and to our parents
Hakarat Hatov for all the love they bestowed on us and for all they taught us
Loving sons
Mr. and Mrs. Bert Pariser
Paul S. Pariser
And All the Pariser Grandchildren

IN MEMORY OF DORA PARISER

Who was born in America, graduated from Long Island University and loved by all.
Together with her husband, Michael Pariser, they embodied the best attributes
of Jewish Americans: family, shul, charity, and America.
Dora's guidelines were:
The glass is always half full.
Be optimistic, be thankful to HaShem and always be a Mentsch.
Those who had the good fortune of knowing Dora Pariser
have been granted the gift of seeing greatness in character.
May we emulate Dora to the best of our abilities.

TABLE OF CONTENTS

PART III: CONTEMPORARY SOCIAL HALACHIC ISSUES

PART IV: GENERAL SHABBAT CONCERNS

PART V: FRONTIERS OF HALACHA

INTRODUCTION

MANY PEOPLE ARE born into a family profession, which over time becomes the pride of the family's older members and the goal of its youth. This describes the occupation of my family, in which the men have been rabbis for the past eighteen generations. My ancestors served communities all over the Jewish world from Spain to Solonika, from Constantinople to Cracow, and many communities in Europe. Fourteen generations ago a famed ancestor, Rav Yosef Katz, served as the rosh yeshiva of the metropolitan city of Cracow for fifty years. He was a brother-in-law of the Rama, the leading rabbinic authority for the customs of Europe.

Each generation was blessed with a son who served as a rabbi in a community. My paternal grandfather, Rav Shmuel ha-Kohen, was the rabbi of Shatava in Kamenetz-Podolsk, Ukraine. His well-known halachic works, including *Minchat Shabbat* on the laws of Shabbat and *Ma'adanei Shemuel* on the laws of Pesach, circulated throughout the Torah world. The Hassidic rabbinate deemed these works invaluable for rendering halachic decisions. My father, Ha-Rav Ha-Gaon R. Meyer Cohen, served as the rabbi of Asbury Park, New Jersey and subsequently as executive director of the Union of Orthodox Rabbis (Agudat HaRabbonim) in the United States and Canada for more than twenty years.

I, too, followed in the family tradition, serving for several years as a pulpit rabbi in West Orange, New Jersey, and then eighteen and a half years as a rabbi of a congregation in Los Angeles, California. After that, I was the *mara de-atra* of the Mizrachi Kehilla in Melbourne, Australia for seven and a half years. I currently serve as rav in West Palm Beach, Florida.

Throughout my rabbinic career, my goals were the four traditional obligations that our sages set before every person: *"Lilmod u-lelamed, lishmor ve-la'asot." "Lilmod"* – the requirement to learn Torah was deemed essential to serving as rav in a community. Throughout my life, I have taken great intellectual joy in simply learning Torah. *"Le-lamed"* – to teach – is what rabbis should do. Torah must be shared and taught to everyone. Although my main forum for teaching Torah consists of classes and lectures, I also use the written word through weekly columns on Halacha published in *The Jewish Press* and other media, and in my books. I have been fortunate that many people have read and enjoyed my creative Torah.

"Lishmor ve-la'asot." Some say that the word *lishmor* relates to prohibitive mitzvot while the word *la'asot* refers to prescriptive ones. The Brisker Rav provides a unique definition for these terms. *La'asot* refers to the observance of both prescriptive and prohibitive mitzvot. A rav must observe the Torah and keep the mitzvot. In addition (*lishmor*), he has a special obligation to guard the *mesorah* – Jewish tradition – ensuring that it will transcend his generation and maintain its strength in the future. Part of the task of guarding Jewish tradition is to see to it that Torah observances are based on Halachic values and not simply upon preventative stringencies.

This suggests that each and every issue must be analyzed in terms of its Halachic components. The mindset of the halachic decisor must be guided by neither stringent nor lenient tendencies. The true guide must be to ascertain the actual law or custom, not whether the result pleases the right or the left wings of the Torah world.

There is another aspect to this. As mentioned, I come from a family of rabbis. In addition, my father-in-law is Ha-Rav ha-Gaon R. Yaakov Nayman, Shlita, a noted disciple of the Brisker Rav. I have many vivid memories of their lives and customs. As a result, I cannot accept the contention by some contemporary rabbis that the Jewish leaders of previous generations were not as pious or as learned as those of the present day.

Torah is universal. It is not rooted in any single country or segment of society, but must be applicable to all countries and all times. It must manifest not the ideology of the European *shtetl* or contemporary American culture. Since its standards come from God, Torah must appear normal, not outlandish or bizarre.

When I am faced with halachic questions, my concern is to first seek out proper rabbinic sources and then to analyze all references through the prism of accepted and impartial halachic principles. I base my final decision upon a process of open-minded Torah research rather than upon a preconceived tendency to be stringent or lenient. The last mishna in Tractate *Uktzin*, the final mishna of the Talmud, states: *"Kol tzaddik ve-tzaddik"* – every single righteous person – will receive a special reward. Commenting on the double usage of the word *tzaddik,* the Tosafot Yom Tov commentary states that it refers to two different types of righteous people, one stringent, the other lenient. God considers both types deserving of reward. Accordingly, the term *tzaddik* refers not only to a scholar whose rulings are stringent but also to the one whose rulings are lenient. Both are proper halachic conclusions.

As a general orientation to a volume devoted to hilchot Shabbat, I should like to quote a statement made by my grandfather in his preface to his work on Shabbat. I have taken the liberty of paraphrasing the contents and expanding certain images slightly.

> Every serious person seeks to impact the world itself; to in some way make a contribution that is lasting [*tikkun olam*]; to perform some action that may have a life of its own even beyond the frail limitation of one's own lifetime. Publishing Torah concepts seems to be a proper vehicle to accomplish this goal, for a quality volume has the potential of influencing future generations. As such, every publication, in a way, is a quest for immortality. Every volume gives an author an opportunity to live again and again in future eras. What a *zechut* [privilege] it is to have one's Torah discussed and even, perhaps, helping to guide future leaders of Israel. For such reasons it is definitely understandable why an author seeks to share thoughts by publication.
>
> At issue is that initial common rabbinical reaction to halachic volumes is to deflate the egos of new authors by questioning their ability and sagacity or even their impudence to suggest that their works or thoughts should be guides for Jewish life. To such critics, I beg of you: do not dismiss the contents without sufficient analysis and thought. Should, after serious deliberations, it be determined that I erred, please inform me in writing of my errors. This will grant me an opportunity, while I have the ability to respond, to review all charges and defend my position. Moreover, after responding to you should I not satisfy your criticism, then I promise, as strength is within me, that in a future publication (for I will continue to write), I will publicly retract all errors I may have committed.
>
> The Chavat Yair writes that should a Torah volume contain but one good Torah thought, it serves as a guard and spiritual protector over the other parts. Hopefully, so it will be with this volume. (*Minchat Shabbat,* Introduction)

Ha-Rav Ha-Gaon R. Naftoli Tzvi Hirsh Berlin (the Netziv, Rosh ha-Yeshivah of the Volozhiner Yeshivah), contended that the highest level of halachic research is the pursuit of halachic creativity – namely, the pursuit of creative responses to contemporary problems (*Meromai Sadeh, Berachot* 8a). This is exactly what this volume is all about. It is a collection of contemporary creative halachic responses to issues and problems that affect modern Jews. I hope that this volume will enable contemporary Jews to understand the rationale of Shabbat observances and thereby increase the joy of Shabbat itself.

Acharon, acharon chaviv: my rebbetzin, Shoshana, has always supported my quest for Torah faithfully. More than anyone else, she constantly encouraged me to learn, teach and write Torah. May God grant her good health and cheer for her devotion, kindness and chessed. She is the epitome of the beloved and honored *"eshet chayil."*

A *birkat Kohen be-ahavah* to our children, grandchildren and great-grandchildren. May God bless you all with health, happiness, success, and continued devotion to Torah.

PART I

KIDDUSH

GUESTS FOR FRIDAY NIGHT KIDDUSH

Question: When guests are invited for Shabbat, is it preferable for one person to make Kiddush for everyone, or should each adult male personally recite Kiddush for himself, his wife, and his family?

Response: The Talmud states: "If people were sitting in the Beit ha-Midrash and light was brought in [at the termination of the Sabbath], Beit Shammai say that each should recite the blessing himself [*bore meorei ha-esh*], while Beit Hillel say that one person should recite the blessing on behalf of everyone because of [the concept of] *be-rov am hadrat melech* (in the multitude of people is the King's glory)" (Proverbs 14:28; *Berachot* 53a).

Based upon this citation, the Vilna Gaon derives a general precept that when a number of people are to perform a mitzvah, it is preferable for one person to recite the blessing for everyone, rather than for each person to recite it separately (Glosses, Ha-Gra, *Orach Chayyim* 8:12).

While the Chayye Adam notes this halachic preference of *be-rov am*, he contends that common usage is for each to recite the blessing on his or her own. The Chayye Adam's rationale for not employing the custom of *be-rov am* is that perhaps most people are simply not knowledgable about the proper procedure for including others in a *berachah*. Such a process requires the person who recites the *berachah* to have intention to include all, while those in attendance must have intention to be so included (*Chayye Adam* Klal 5:17; also cited by the *Mishna Berurah, Orach Chayyim* 8:13).

The *Aruch ha-Shulchan* rules, for example, that when several people put on their *tallitot* each morning, it is halachically preferable for one of them to recite the *berachah* for everyone because of the concept of *be-rov am*. He notes, however, that common custom is for each to recite his own *berachah* because, in that instance, it is difficult to synchronize the process so that everyone puts on their *tallitot* simultaneously after the *berachah* (*Orach Chayyim* 8:11).

Accordingly, in a situation when no action is mandatory, and those present and the head of the household observes the proper process of *kavannah* (to be *motzi* and *yotze*), then one person should make Kiddush for everyone.

Interestingly, the *Shulchan Aruch ha-Rav* adds an important halachic point. He contends that whether the person recites the blessing for everyone or each person recites it for himself is a matter of personal preference and that each option is equally valid. Though halacha generally grants preference to the concept of *be-rov am*, he rules that a person cannot be compelled to fulfill a mitzvah in this way. His argument is that when one person includes another in the recitation of his blessing, the person who recites the blessing becomes the other's surrogate (*shaliah*). Therefore, one cannot oblige a person to observe a mitzvah via a surrogate when he wishes to do so himself (*Orach Chayyim* 213:6). In other words, since it is generally preferable to perform a mitzvah by oneself rather than through a surrogate, such a concern may militate against the option of permitting one person the honor of including everyone in his *berachah*. However, it may be demonstrated that there is a procedure in which the logical arguments of the *Shulchan Aruch ha-Rav* do not apply.

The Rambam rules that one may fulfill the obligation for a *berachah* even without the response of "amen" provided that the listener heard the entire *berachah* and had the intention to be included in it. Moreover, he adds that whoever responds "amen" after the blessing is considered to have recited the blessing itself.

The Kesef Mishneh was troubled with this halacha. Why is it necessary to respond "amen" at all? If the rule is that merely by listening attentively one is considered as having recited the berachah (*shome'a ke-oneh*), then what is the value of saying "amen"? The Kesef Mishneh answers that when one does not say "amen", one may not be compared to the person who made the blessing (Rambam, *Hilchot Berachot* 1:11).

The meaning may be as follows. When one recites a blessing for others who listen, the reciter becomes the listeners' surrogate. Yet when the listeners respond "amen", they are considered as having recited the blessing themselves. In other words, the response of "amen" is considered equivalent to reciting the blessing. Add to this the idea that responding "amen" is considered greater than making a *berachah* (*Berachot* 53b).

Even the *Shulchan Aruch ha-Rav* would agree that when everyone responds "amen" to the Kiddush that is chanted by the head of the household, for example, then it is as if each one present had recited it themselves. Thus, in this instance, it is probable that all authorities would agree that preference should be granted to one person to recite kiddush on behalf of everyone (*be-rov am*) rather than for each to make Kiddush on his own. All those present should have proper intent and answer "amen".

FRIDAY NIGHT KIDDUSH: THE OPENING PHRASE

Question: How does one begin the Friday night Kiddush? What is the proper wording or phrase that should be recited at the beginning of this prayer?

Response: Though Kiddush is a popular mitzvah that is observed every Friday evening, its actual introductory phrase is not clear.

The Tur states explicitly that Kiddush begins with the recitation of *"Va-yechulu,"* the first word of Scripture's three-verse account of the Sabbath of Creation. *"Va-yechulu ha-shamayim"* – heaven was completed (Genesis 2:1–3; see also the *Tur Shulchan Aruch, Orach Chayyim* 271). Therefore, the Kiddush is comprised of three distinct yet interrelated segments:

An introduction composed of Biblical verses recalling the Sabbath of Creation.

A blessing over wine.

A blessing sanctifying Shabbat.

Indeed, the *Va-yechulu* excerpt is reserved for Friday night. The Codes note that if one did not recite Kiddush on Friday night, one may recite it on Shabbat itself. The Rama notes that this law does not refer to the *Va-yechulu* portion, which is not chanted in the daytime (*Orach Chayyim* 271:8). The Taz suggests that the reason for this is that creation was concluded at night (*Orach Chayyim* 271:11). The Vilna Gaon cites the Talmud (*Shabbat* 119b) as the source for this law. The implication is that the Talmud mentions instances showing that it is meritorious to recite *Va-yechulu* on Friday night. The fact that the Talmud specifically notes its recitation only on Friday night probably indicates that there is no obligation to recite it on Shabbat.

Yet the common custom on Friday night is to precede the Kiddush with the words *yom ha-shishi* – "the sixth day." According to the Rama, the reason that this phrase is included is that the first Hebrew letters of these two words, *yud* and *heh,* together with the first letters of the phrase that occurs afterwards, *Va-yechulu ha-shamayim* – *vav* and *heh* – spell out the four-letter Divine Name (*Orach Chayyim* 271:10). When the Rama introduced this custom in his commentary on the Tur, he contended that it was practiced by the *medakdekim* – people who are scrupulous in observance (see *Darchei Moshe, Orach Chayyim* 271). The Codes of Rav Yosef Caro do not mention it. Accordingly, it appears that Sephardim, who generally follow Rav Yosef Caro, started Kiddush with *Va-yechulu*. Some pious Ashkenazim began reciting the words *yom ha-shishi*. Subsequently, all Ashkenizm accepted the concept and also chanted *yom ha-shishi* on Friday night. In other words, a phrase was added to the Kiddush not for its inherent meaning but simply because it spells out a Divine Name.

The Vilna Gaon suggests that reciting the words *yom ha-shishi* recognizes the principle of *tosefet Shabbat* – extending Shabbat by including part of the previous weekday text as an integral portion of it (see *Be'urei ha-Gra, Orach Chayyim* 271:26). Thus, Kiddush reflects the fact that Shabbat marks the sanctification of the weekday.

The difficulty is that the words *yom ha-shishi,* which are the last words of the verse preceding the paragraph that begins with *Va-yechulu,* are the last quoted words of a sentence. Apart from the symbolism noted above, it is bizarre to begin with the words of a previous verse that seem irrelevant to the sentence structure of the successive verses. To resolve this problem somewhat, the introductory part of Kiddush was expanded to begin with the phrase *"Va-yehi erev va-yehi voker, yom ha-shishi"* – "it was evening and it was morning, the sixth day" (Genesis 1:31). This custom recognizes that the words *yom ha-shishi* by themselves are meaningless intheir partial appearance.

The difficulty is that such a process still goes against the tradition of citing half-verses of Scripture. The general rule is that we may not give new endings to Biblical verses, which must conclude exactly as they are in the Bible. This means the one should not cite a partial scriptural verse (*"kol pasuk de-lo pesak Moshe," Berachot* 12b).

The *Aruch ha-Shulchan* cites a custom to begin Kiddush silently with the words *"Va-yar Elohim et kol asher asah ve-hineh tov me'od: va-yehi erev, va-yehi voker"* and then to continue aloud with *"yom ha-shishi."* The reason is that one should recite complete Scriptural verses. The Aruch ha-Shulchan concludes that this is a proper custom (*Orach Chayyim* 271:25).

In a discussion of Kiddush for Shabbat morning, the Aruch ha-Shulchan rules that it is not against halacha to preface the Kiddush with the phrase *"Al ken berach,"* which is half of a scriptural verse (Exodus 20:11). Indeed, he notes that it is permitted to chant a partial verse as long as one has the intention of preceding a blessing with a phrase rather than specifically citing Scripture (*Orach Chayyim* 289:3). This suggests that the Aruch HaShulchan merely notes a preference for citing complete verses, but does not invalidate or prohibit the use of partial ones.

Indeed, the *Mishna Berurah* makes no comment concerning the proper introduction to the Friday night Kiddush. This is somewhat unusual because this work specifically rules that one should not begin the Shabbat morning Kiddush with the phrase *Al ken berach* because it is the middle of a verse. Indeed, he specifically says that to begin Kiddush with the words *Al ken berach* is against Halacha (*Ke-neged ha-din* 289:2). Now, if it is prohibited to cite only a partial verse on Shabbat morning, it is logical to assume that the Mishna Berurah would hold the same view for the entire day. Yet he does not note this issue at all concerning Friday night Kiddush.

The Chatam Sofer discusses the issue, suggesting a reason why people do not begin Kiddush on Friday night with the beginning of the verse *Va-yar*. The Midrash notes that the phrase *tov me'od* – "very good" – refers to death. Accordingly, Jews simply did not wish to begin Kiddush with a phrase that related to death (Responsum *Orach Chayyim* 10).

This may be the rationale for the Mishna Berurah's omission of the problem as it relates to Friday night. One should always seek to recite complete verses. Accordingly, the Shabbat morning Kiddush should contain only complete Scriptural verses. Yet when the complete verse may have negative overtones, such as death, then perhaps there is nothing wrong with reciting a partial verse. In other words, as long as there is no negative contrary tradition, one should recite complete verses. It is obvious that the Aruch ha-Shulchan believes that such negative associations have no effect upon actual halachic concerns.

THE FUNCTION OF "VA-YECHULU HA-SHAMAYIM"

Question: At the Friday night Kiddush, does the recitation of the Biblical verses detailing the story of Shabbat Bereshit (*"Va-yechulu ha-shamayim"*) relate to any halachic aspect of Kiddush? Is there a significant element of Kiddush within the Biblical verses that is lacking in the standardized format of the blessings of Kiddush?

Response: Ha-Rav Baruch Dov Povarsky, Rosh ha-Yeshivah of Ponevezh, Bnai Brak, noted the following distinction between the mitzvah of recalling the Exodus from Egypt throughout the year and the special mitzvah to remember the Exodus from Egypt on the eve of Pesach. He contended that the general mitzvah to recall the Exodus throughout the year is a mandate to remember the phenomenon of the Exodus itself. There is no requirement to note the specific date of the Exodus. It is not necessary to state that the Exodus took place on the fifteenth day of Nisan. Similarly, the mitzvah to recall the war with Amalek does not stipulate any obligation to cite the day or month that the incident took place. One observes the mitzvah simply by recalling that it happened.

However, on the eve of Pesach, the obligation is more detailed. The Torah specifically states: "Remember this day which you departed from Egypt" (Exodus 13:3). Hence, it is not enough to recall the general fact of the Exodus. It is necessary to know the actual day that the Exodus took place: the night of the fifteenth of Nisan. This may also be the response to the question in the Haggadah, *"Ma nishtana ha-laila ha-zeh* – Why is this night different?" Namely (*Sefer Bad Kodesh,* Parshat Bo), why do we need to remember the night of the fifteenth of Nisan?

We should recall that the commandment to remember Shabbat is comparable to the commandment to recall the Exodus on Pesach. Pertaining to the mitzvah of Shabbat, the Torah states, *"Zachor et yom ha-shabbat –* Remember the Shabbat day" (Exodus 20:8). In other words, the command is not only to remember Shabbat but also to recall the day of Shabbat. This suggests that on Shabbat we must recall that it is the seventh day of the week. To say merely that it was Shabbat did not meet the Biblical requirement. The Kiddush blessing does not specify that Shabbat is the seventh day of the week. The only reference to the fact that the Jewish Shabbat is the seventh day of the week occurs in the Biblical account of Shabbat Bereshit, which notes this in the verses that begins *"Va-yechulu ha-shamayim."* Note the following: "On the seventh day, God completed His work that He had done, and He abstained on the seventh day from all His work which He had done. G-d blessed the seventh day and sanctified it" (Genesis 2:2, 3, Artscroll translation). Therefore, the Biblical verses were made part of the Kiddush in order to fulfill the obligation to state that Shabbat is the seventh day of the week.

RECITING BLESSING FOR WINE AFTER KIDDUSH

Question: On Friday night, the head of the household made Kiddush for everyone at the meal and then distributed portions of wine. Should each person recite the blessing over wine independently before drinking?

Response: The Talmud notes a debate between Beit Shammai and Beit Hillel concerning the proper sequence of the Friday night Kiddush. Beit Shammai contends that the blessing over wine should be preceded by the blessing over the day of Shabbat. Beit Hillel disagrees, saying that on Friday night the blessing over wine should precede the blessing over Shabbat itself (*Berachot* 51b).

Ha-Rav Yaakov of Lissa (see *Derech ha-Chayyim*) rules that those who recite the blessing over wine in such a case demonstrate that they accept the blessing over Shabbat as recited by the host, but not the blessing over wine. Accordingly, by reciting the blessing over wine independently, they are openly following the ruling of Beit Shammai rather than that of Beit Hillel. Because Halacha accords with the Beit Hillel's position in this case, no one should recite the blessing independently. This means that when wine is given to those who heard Kiddush, they should drink without reciting a further blessing.

MAKING KIDDUSH FOR WOMEN

Question: Is it proper for men to recite *Kiddush* on behalf of their wives on Friday night?

Response: The *Magen Avraham* ruled that the Biblical mitzvah of sanctifying the Shabbat (*Zachor et yom ha-Shabbat*) is fulfilled during the Friday evening prayers. Both the necessity for wine and the rule that Kiddush should immediately precede a meal are rabbinic ordinances (*Shuclhan Aruch, Orach Chayyim* 271:1).

To this R. Yechezkel Landau (ibid., Commentary *Dagul Merevava*) noted that women generally do not recite *Maariv*. Therefore, the men – who do recite it – are obligated to recite Kiddush by rabbinical rule, while the women have yet to fulfill their scriptural mitzvah. If so, he asked, how are the men able to include their wives in the Kiddush that they recite at home when the women's level of obligation is stronger? Accordingly, he ruled that it is questionable whether men who have already fulfilled their mitzvah should chant the Kiddush on behalf of their wives, who have not yet fulfilled their mitzvah.

In an attempt to explain why men may make Kiddush for their wives, the *Mishna Berurah* (*Orach Chayyim* 271:2) stated that most people simply do not have the intention of observing the mitzvah of Kiddush at the synagogue. Therefore, the status of both the men and women is equal and a husband may recite Kiddush for his wife.

Scripture states: "Remember the Sabbath to keep it holy" (*zachor et yom ha-Shabbat le-kaddesho*, Exodus 20:8). Tradition has it that a verbal statement suffices to meet the requirement of observance. Yet the minimum phrase that must be recited is not clear. R. Akiva Eiger contended that the greeting *Shabbat Tovah* ("Good Shabbat") may be enough to satisfy the Biblical requirement. The *Mishna Berurah* questioned this formula by noting that the Rambam provides an extended format ruling, "It is a positive scriptural mitzvah to sanctify the Shabbat with words, as it is written, 'Remember the Sabbath to keep it holy'; that is, remember it with praise and sanctification" (Rambam, *Laws of Shabbat* 29:1; see *Bi'ur Halacha, Orach Chayyim* 271). Thus, it is not enough simply to remember the Sabbath on the seventh day. One must also praise and sanctify it. Accordingly, the *Mishna Berurah* concluded that the phrase "Good Shabbat" lacked the element of sanctification. In addition, the *Mishna Berurah* suggested that the scriptural mitzvah may require reference to the Exodus from Egypt.

Yet the Ramban contended that one may observe this mitzvah on every day of the week by referring to its relationship to Shabbat. The first day is not called Sunday but the first day of Shabbat; Monday, the second day of Shabbat; and so on throughout the week. Thus, one constantly recalls Shabbat. Moreover, the mandate of sanctification is that Shabbat must be noted on the day of Shabbat itself. Just as the Jubilee year requires a formal proclamation by the *beit din* that it is holy, so, too, "is it necessary to recall Shabbat when we sanctify it" (Commentary, Exodus 20:8). This suggests that the mandate of *le-kaddesho* ("to keep it holy") is a requirement to verbalize a statement on Shabbat itself and not necessarily to recite a statement of sanctification.

For men, the *Maariv* prayer meets the Biblical requirement, while for women, perhaps the blessing over the Friday night candles is also a form of sanctifying the Shabbat. In Leviticus (19:2), Scripture states: *kedoshim tiheyu,* "You shall be holy," and the Ramban noted that the *Torat Kohanim* defined this concept by the statement *perushim tiheyu,* "You shall be separate." Thus *kedushah* refers to that which is separate, distinct, and unique. By a process of lighting candles and reciting a blessing, women formally acknowledge the sanctity of Shabbat. Indeed, the blessing itself mentions *kedushah,* which should meet both the Rambam's and the Ramban's requirements. This then should place the obligation upon women on an equal footing with that upon men. Indeed, R. Meir Arik rules that the extra prayers women recite after lighting candles on Friday night fulfill the scriptural mitzvah of Kiddush (*Responsa Imrei Yosher* 1:202).

DIFFERENCES BETWEEN THE KIDDUSH OF MEN & WOMEN

Question: Is there a distinction between men and women regarding the mitzvah of reciting Kiddush on Friday night?

Response: Research indicates that some rabbinic authorities have, indeed, postulated qualitative distinctions between men and women regarding the mitzvah of Kiddush. The following Talmudic text, from *Berachot* 51b, is crucial to an understanding of the issue:

> Beit Shammai says the blessing is first said over the [sanctity of] the day and then over the wine, because
>
> 1. It is on account of the day that the wine is used, and [moreover]
> 2. The day has already become holy before the wine has been brought.

Beit Hillel says that a blessing is said over the wine first and then over the day: *peri ha-gafen* followed by *mekaddesh ha-Shabbat* because the wine provides the occasion for the sanctification. Another explanation is that the blessing over wine is said regularly while the blessing of the day is said only at infrequent weekly intervals, and the mitzvah that is observed with greater frequency always takes preference over those that are observed less often. The halacha is as laid down by the ruling of Beit Hillel. What is the point of the "other explanation"? – In case you should say that there (in the explanation of Beit Shammai's view) that two reasons are presented, while here (in explanation of Beit Hillel's) only one, then we reply that there are two here also (the second one being that) the blessing over wine is more frequent and the blessing over the day of Shabbat is less so, and a mitzvah which is observed more frequently (*tadir*) takes precedence over one that is observed less frequently.

Rav Yechezkel Landau (the rav of Prague) posed two pertinent questions to the position of Beit Hillel.

The consensus of halachic authorities is that the scriptural mandate of Kiddush is observed without wine. Thus, a person in a desert who has no way to obtain wine is still obligated to sanctify the Shabbat. If this is so, then Beit Hillel's theory that "the wine provides the occasion for saying the sanctification" has no validity, for Shabbat must be sanctified with or without wine.

The blessing over Shabbat is the observance of a scriptural mitzvah. Consequently, it should have priority over the blessing over wine, which is only a rabbinic mandate, even though the latter is more frequent.

As a result of such concerns, R. Landau ruled that the debate between Beit Shammai and Beit Hillel related only to rabbinic observances. The scriptural mitzvah was not germane to the debate because it was already fulfilled during the Friday evening prayers. However, if the scriptural mitzvah was not fulfilled before Kiddush, then the halacha would accord with Beit Shammai's procedure. Therefore, R. Landau noted, this suggests a novel halachic practice relating to women. Since women generally do not recite the Friday evening prayers, their scriptural mitzvah (see *Berachot* 20b) still applies during the Kiddush before the Shabbat meal. Thus women should follow the practice of Beit Shammai by reciting first the blessing of Shabbat and subsequently the blessing over wine (*Tzelach* – commentary *Berachot* 51b). Women do not follow this ruling. Perhaps a reason why the practice is for men to always recite Kiddush for women (despite the possibility existing that the women may have a greater obligation) is to retain a sense of unity and cohesion in the order of Kiddush in the home.

WOMEN RECITING KIDDUSH
FOR HER HUSBAND AND FAMILY

Question: May a woman recite Kiddush in her home on Friday night on behalf of her husband and family?

Response: For the purpose of this discussion, I am assuming that both husband and wife are knowledgeable and able to recite Kiddush. The concern is whether a family may on occasion give the honor of reciting Kiddush to the woman rather than to the man. Is this contrary to Halacha?

The Talmud notes that women as well as men are required to say Kiddush. Indeed, it is deemed a scriptural mitzvah for both (*Berachot* 20b). Accordingly, since both are equally obliged to recite Kiddush from a Biblical viewpoint, women may make Kiddush for their husbands just as their husbands may make Kiddush for their wives. From a pragmatic view, however, there appears to be a negative rabbinical attitude to women who perform mitzvot on their husbands' behalf. The Talmud specifically states that women may recite the grace after meals for themselves as well as for their husbands, yet the rabbis felt that it was not proper. Indeed, they commented, "Let a curse come upon a man whose his wife and children recite the blessing for him" (*Berachot* 20b).

Although this suggests that the rabbis did not accept the idea of women reciting scripturally-mandated blessings for men, this is not the reason for their attitude. They were expressing their disapproval of a situation in which the husband was ignorant and could only fulfill the mitzvah of Kiddush if his wife or children recited it for him. However, in a case where both husband and wife are able to recite the prayer, the rabbis' negative attitude does not apply. Indeed, the ArtScroll translation explains that the reason for the rabbis' negative attitude was the husband's ignorance and inability to recite Kiddush for himself. It appears that there is no halachic problem with a husband and wife taking turns reciting the Friday night Kiddush.

However, a review of one of the responsa of Rav Akiva Eiger, *z"l*, uncovers a possible halachic problem with women making Kiddush for men. The basis for the position that women have a scriptural commandment to recite Kiddush is that there are two Biblical commandments that pertain to

Shabbat: *Zachor* (Remember Shabbat – Exodus 20:8) and *Shamor* (Keep or observe Shabbat – Deut. 5:12). The former is the mitzvah of Kiddush, while the latter relates to all the prohibitions of Shabbat. The Talmud rules, "Whoever is included in the commandment to keep Shabbat is also included in the command to remember Shabbat." Since women are obligated to observe the prohibitions of Shabbat, they are also included in the prescriptive commandment to recite Kiddush. Accordingly, even though Kiddush is observed in a specific time frame and women are not obligated in such mitzvot, they must recite Kiddush because of the special Biblical connection of *zachor* to *shamor* (*Berachot* 20b).

Interestingly, the relationship of *zachor* to *shamor* could have been interpreted differently. Instead of saying that whoever was obligated in one is also obligated in the other, the Talmud could have said that whoever is *not* obligated to observe one is also not obligated to observe the other. In other words, since women were not required to recite Kiddush because this is done only at a specific time, they also were not required to observe the prohibitions of Shabbat. According to our commentaries, the reason that we do not use this lenient method of interpreting the relationship of the verses is because of the accepted rule that where a relationship of Biblical verses (a *hekesh*) is concerned, only the stringent interpretation is used and has halachic merit.

The following question was posed to Rav Akiva Eiger, *z"l*: What is the meaning of the general rule that when we interpret relationships between scriptural verses, we accept only the stringent position? Is it because this is the essential rule for interpreting verse relationships, or is it based on the general concept that in matters of doubt about scriptural mitzvot, one is stringent (*safek de-oraita le-chumra*)? Rav Eiger's position was that the stringency was due to the nature of the rule and the tradition of interpreting verse relationships, not due to doubt. (See *Kovetz Responsa Rabbi Akiva Eiger*, Volume II, *Teshuvot ve-chiddushei Rabbenu Akiva Eiger* 17.)

According to the position that women must recite Kiddush because of doubt pertaining to a scriptural mitzvah, as posed but rejected by Rav Eiger, it would not be proper for women to recite Kiddush for men who are obligated to perform the mitzvah without any questions about the status of the obligation itself. Since Rav Eiger ruled against this position, it would appear that women may recite Kiddush for men, even according to Rav Eiger.

The Mishna Berurah states that the Taz, Magen Avraham and the Vilna Gaon permit women to recite Kiddush for men (*Orach Chayyim* 271:4). Indeed, he rules that in matters pertaining to Kiddush, "women are equal to men." In *Shaar ha-Tzion* (note 8), he adds that this is contrary to the views of the Rashal and Bach, who are stringent in this matter.

The Mishna Berurah makes a suggestion about the practice of women reciting Kiddush for men. He states, "*Ab initio* one should be stringent and not permit a woman to recite Kiddush for men who are not part of her family because this lacks proper respect and dignity" (*zila milta*). In other words, while it does not violate Halacha, it is improper. Yet if a woman made Kiddush for a man who is not a member of her household, the Kiddush, post facto, would fulfill the halachic requirement.

What I find fascinating is the case that the Mishna Berurah fails to mention overtly. He simply does not discuss a case of a woman making Kiddush for her husband. The clear implication is that a woman may do so even *lechatchila*. Indeed, the Mishna Berurah does not even mention that such an act is improper. It is only when a woman recites Kiddush for a man who is not a member of her family that it is considered improper by some.

THE FRIDAY NIGHT KIDDUSH
IN THE SYNAGOGUE

Question: Why is Kiddush recited in some synagogues before the conclusion of religious services on Friday nights?

Response: The Talmud notes that Kiddush must be recited immediately before the Sabbath meal. If so, the question is asked, "Why do we recite Kiddush on Friday evening in the synagogue?" (Since worshippers leave in order to eat in their own homes, the synagogue Kiddush is a violation of that rule.) The response is that this Kiddush was designed for guests who would be staying overnight in the synagogue and eating there (*Pesachim* 101a). Consequently, Rabbenu Asher concluded that when people do not have the custom of eating in the synagogue on Friday evening, the recitation of this Kiddush is a form of taking God's name in vain and should be discontinued. Rabbenu Yona noted that the requirement to recite Kiddush before the Sabbath meal is a rabbinic ordinance. As a result, since there are people who do not know how to make Kiddush, the custom developed to recite it in the synagogue in order to permit such people to fulfill the scriptural mitzvah. Rabbenu Asher countered this position by saying that the rule prohibiting Kiddush unless it is immediately before a meal means that such a Kiddush is invalid (See Beit Yosef, *Tur Shulchan Aruch, Orach Chayyim* 269). Rabbenu Yona's position is that the rabbinic rules do not cancel out the scriptural mitzvah.

Rabbenu Yona's position has merit. What can be wrong with giving people an opportunity to fulfill the scriptural mitzvah even if this means that they do not fulfill the rabbinic one?

Moreover, the custom of reciting Kiddush in the synagogue on Friday nights has a history of over two thousand years of uninterrupted practice. An additional factor is the kabbalistic tradition noted by the Tur Shulchan Aruch that the Friday night Kiddush in synagogue is a *segula* for healing the eyes (see Tur, *Shulchan Aruch* 269).

THE PERMITTED LENGTH OF TIME BETWEEN KIDDUSH AND THE SHABBAT MEAL

Question: It is well known that Kiddush on Shabbat must take place at a meal. Should one be concerned with the amount of time that lapses between the recitation of Kiddush and the Shabbat meal?

Response: The halacha is *"Ein Kiddush ela be-makom seuda."* In other words, the mitzvah of Kiddush applies only when the Kiddush is recited at the time and place of a meal. If Kiddush was recited and no meal was eaten afterwards, the mitzvah of Kiddush was not fulfilled. The Rama notes that one should begin eating *le-altar* in the place where the Kiddush was recited (*Orach Chayyim* 273:3). At issue is the definition of the Hebrew word *le-altar,* which generally means "right away."

The Mishna Berurah rules that one should not delay the meal even briefly. Though some authorities maintain one may go outside his home for a short while and then return to the place where Kiddush was recited, others disagree, ruling that Kiddush must be recited again. The Mishna Berurah rules that initially, one should be stringent in this matter. Post facto, however, one who answers a call of nature need not recite Kiddush again (*Mishna Berurah* 273:12). The implication appears to be that any delay not due to a call of nature between Kiddush and the meal is not permitted and that in such a case Kiddush must be recited again when the meal begins. This insistence upon having the meal immediately after Kiddush may be the source for the German Jewish (and some others') custom to wash one's hands, make Kiddush and then recite the blessing over bread, which begins the meal, which guarantees that the meal will be intertwined with the Kiddush.

The Aruch ha-Shulchan provides a less rigid ruling on these issues. He contends that the word *le-altar* does not mean immediately, but rather, shortly, without much delay. He substantiates this position by noting that Halacha permits one to recite Kiddush in a hall downstairs and to eat upstairs on another floor providing that this was the intention when he recited Kiddush. The amount of time that the person who made Kiddush has to spend walking upstairs is not enough to warrant a second recitation of

Kiddush. Indeed, the Aruch ha-Shulchan notes that many have the custom to change their clothes for the meal after having made Kiddush. He concludes by stating that the Torah was not given to angels, implying that Halacha must consider normal human concerns and behavior (*Aruch ha-Shulchan* 273:4).

THE PROXIMITY OF KIDDUSH
TO THE SHABBAT MEAL

Question: The rule is that Kiddush must be recited where one eats one's meal. What are the physical dimensions to this concept? Must one know the exact place where the Shabbat meal must be eaten when one recites Kiddush?

Response: The *Aruch ha-Shulchan,* which discusses this issue in detail, rules as follows:

When a person makes Kiddush, he need not know the exact spot where he will be eating, providing it is within the same room, even if the room is a great hall. In addition, one may recite Kiddush in one room and eat in another providing that during his recitation he can see the place where he will be eating, even if only through a window (*Shulchan Aruch, Orach Chayyim* 273:2).

If a person makes Kiddush in one room but will be eating in another room that he cannot see during his recitation, he must have the *kavanna* (intention) of eating there as he recites Kiddush. In this case, the place where he will be eating his meal should be located in the same building, even if it is on another floor (273:3).

However, if the meal is scheduled to take place in a home or building other than in the place where he recited Kiddush, he must eat a minimum amount (a *ke-zayit,* or olive's weight) of *mezonot* in order to validate his recitation. If he has no *mezonot*, then the Kiddush is invalid and he must recite Kiddush again at the meal itself (273:3).

FOOD AND DRINK ON SHABBAT BEFORE KIDDUSH

Question: It is well known that one may not eat or drink before reciting Kiddush on Shabbat morning. So why do many religious people drink coffee and eat cake on Shabbat morning before going to synagogue?

Response: The prohibition against eating or drinking before Kiddush on Shabbat applies during the period of time that one is obligated to recite Kiddush. It does not apply at other times. The general halacha is that on Shabbat morning the obligation to recite Kiddush does not apply before prayer (*Mishna Berurah,* 89:23; *Aruch ha-Shulchan, Orach Chayyim* 289:4) Therefore, since there is no obligation to recite Kiddush prior to prayer, there is no prohibition on eating or drinking.

Rav Shlomo Kluger posits a novel addendum to the above rule. He contends that on Shabbat morning there is no obligation to recite Kiddush before prayer as long as one recited Kiddush on Friday night. In such a case, the Shabbat morning obligation does not apply until after prayer. One who did not make Kiddush on Friday night is still under the obligation, on Shabbat morning, to recite the blessings of the Friday night Kiddush. In this case, one may not eat or drink even early on Shabbat morning before reciting the Friday night Kiddush (Responsa *Ha-elef lecha Shlomo, Orach Chayyim* 121).

From when does the mitzvah of Kiddush on Shabbat morning apply?

The *Aruch ha-Shulchan* suggests that the entire mitzvah of Kiddush on Shabbat morning is a form of regard for the Shabbat meal. He asks: if the Biblical mitzvah was fulfilled on Friday night, then why did the rabbis impose an obligation to recite Kiddush once again on Shabbat morning? He notes that the purpose is to enhance the Shabbat meal (*Aruch ha-Shulchan* 289:1). Since we have a general rule that Kiddush is recited only at a meal (*Kiddush be-makom seuda*), then the mitzvah applies only when a full meal may be eaten.

Of interest is the exact period of time that the Shabbat morning Kiddush commences. Is it after Shacharit or after Musaf? To the extent that Kiddush may only be recited at a meal, those who permit Kiddush after Shacharit would also permit a meal. The downside to this position would be that unless Kiddush is said after Shacharit, no food (candy) may be eaten. If, on the other hand the position is that Kiddush does not start till after Musaf, then, one may have some candy even without reciting Kiddush prior to Musaf.

In considering the halachic status of each position, the Aruch ha-Shulchan notes that the Talmud records that Birkat Kohanim is recited at Mussaf services because at that time of the day, people are generally not under the influence of alcohol (*Ta'anit* 26a). The Tur argues that this citation is proof that Jews did not eat full meals, which included alcoholic drinks, before Mussaf. Otherwise, Birkat Kohanim would not be allowed at Mussaf. One refutation is that eating a meal before Mussaf was not prohibited; it was simply not customary to eat a full meal and be under the influence of alcohol at that time. The Aruch ha-Shulchan concludes that the custom is not to allow full meals before Mussaf (*Aruch ha-Shulchan, Orach Chayyim* 286:13).

The Mishna Berurah rules that the time of Kiddush falls after *Shacharit* (286:7). The Ba'er Hetev cites the Rashal, who maintains that the mitzvah of Kiddush applies after Mussaf (*Orach Chayyim* 89:12), and similarly the Be'er Moshe cites many sages who maintain that Kiddush does not commence till after *Musaf* and accordingly it is permissible to taste some food prior to *Musaf.* Indeed some scholars even contend that anyone who rules that it is prohibited to taste food before *Musaf* is contrary to the general accepted minhag. (Be'er Moshe Orach Chayyim 286:3). The custom today is not to eat a full meal before Mussaf on Shabbat.

Thus, anyone who wishes to rely on the concept that Kiddush may be recited only after Mussaf, when a full meal may be eaten, and therefore eats candy without making Kiddush beforehand, may rely upon several Rabbinic authorities. This is the halachic rationale (*melamed zechut*) regarding those who eat sweets at bar mitzvahs and aufrufs before Kiddush.

A LEFT-HANDED PERSON HOLDING THE KIDDUSH GOBLET

Question: Should a left-handed person hold the Kiddush cup in his left hand during Kiddush?

Response: The *Shulchan Aruch* notes that a left-handed person should hold the goblet in his left hand, contrary to the practice of right-handed people, who hold the goblet in their right hand (*Orach Chayyim* 183:5). However, the Taz contends that for rabbinic mitzvot one should make no distinction between right-handed and left-handed people. All should follow the most prevalent mode, which is to use the right hand (*Orach Chayyim* 183:9). Neither the Mishna Berurah nor the *Aruch ha-Shulchan* cites this position of the Taz.

The Taz bases his view on the halachic position that even a left-handed person should hold the *lulav* and *etrog* in his right hand because the actual requirement of which hand to hold these in is not of scriptural origin. However, since the Rama rules that a left-handed person should hold the *lulav* in his left hand (*Orach Chayyim* 651:3), the same should be the correct procedure for holding a goblet of wine used to fulfill a mitzvah.

The Vilna Gaon notes that while the above concerns are ways to enhance the mitzvah (*hiddur mitzvah*), they do not require repetition of the *berachah* (*Mishna Berurah* 183:20). Therefore, even if one held the Kiddush cup in a way that is less preferred in halacha, the blessing is still valid.

THE TEXT OF THE SHABBAT MORNING KIDDUSH

Question: Many have the custom of reciting half of a Biblical verse prior to the blessing of wine for Kiddush on Shabbat morning: *"Al ken berach Hashem et yom ha-Shabbat va-yekadshehu"* (Therefore God blessed the seventh day and sanctified it"). This is a partial verse – the second part of Exodus 20:11. Why, of all the scriptural verses in the Bible that mention the sanctity of Shabbat, do we use a verse fragment?

Response: A review of a different section of the *Shulchan Aruch* that does not deal directly with the mitzvah of Kiddush sheds light on this issue.

The Shulchan Aruch rules as follows: "Written words of the Torah may not be recited by heart" (*Orach Chayyim* 49:1). The *Mishna Berurah* notes that many scholars, including the Vilna Gaon, contend that this principle is applicable only to cases where one recites Biblical verses to include others in a mitzvah (49:2).

A prime example of citing Biblical verses to include others in a mitzvah (in other words to fulfill the obligation on their behalf) is to make Kiddush on Shabbat also on behalf of members of one's family, or for a rav to recite Kiddush on behalf of the members of the congregation.

The principle of not reciting Biblical verses by heart may be the reason why the custom of using only half of a verse for Kiddush became popular. People did not wish to have to search for a siddur in order to recite Kiddush for their families. Therefore, they felt that reciting half a verse would not violate the prohibition against reciting Biblical verses by heart. Indeed, the Mishna Berurah concludes that although there are several lenient views regarding reciting verses from memory, one should be stringent about doing so when one includes others in a mitzvah (49:6).

This analysis suggests that should one recite several verses for the Shabbat Kiddush [Isaiah 58:13–14 (*"Im tashiv"*), Exodus 31:16–17 (*"Ve-shamru"*) or Exodus 20:8–11 (*"Zachor"*)], then one should consult a siddur rather than recite these verses from memory.

KIDDUSH ON SHABBAT MORNING
AT THE SYNAGOGUE

Question: Is it proper to recite Kiddush at synagogues on Shabbat morning, as is customary in a large number of synagogues?

Response: The general rule is that where one does not eat a meal then one may not recite Kiddush (see *Pesachim* 101a and *Shulchan Aruch* 273:1).

At issue is the practice in synagogues all over the world to serve food after services. The common practice is that the rav makes Kiddush, after which the congregants eat various snack foods while standing. This is not considered a Shabbat meal, and indeed, most return home to eat their Shabbat meal afterwards. Since no formal meal is eaten, may Kiddush still be recited and the snack foods eaten?

The answer is to provide a halachic definition of a minimum meal. The Mishna Berurah rules that one may recite Kiddush as long as one drinks a *revi'it* of wine or eats an amount of bread or cake the size of an olive. Thus, other liquids such as beer would not meet this requirement. Also, if one should eat only fruit, the Kiddush would not be valid. The *Mishna Berurah* distinguishes between someone who makes Kiddush only for himself and one who is reciting it on the behalf of others. If one makes Kiddush for other people, then unless he ate a *ke-zayit* of cake, it is not considered that Kiddush took place and a meal eaten even if he drank more than a *revi'it* of wine. If one is weak and no cake is available, some authorities rule that one may rely on those sages who maintain that fruit on Shabbat is considered a meal. Yet even this leniency is limited to Shabbat morning and not Friday night, and to those who do not feel well (*Mishna Berurah* 273:22, 25, 26). Some authorities contend that one must drink a *revi'it* of wine in addition to that used for Kiddush (see *Shaarei ha-Tzion* 273:29).

Thus, anyone who makes Kiddush for others on Shabbat morning should make certain to eat a *ke-zayit* of cake. Otherwise, the halachic validity of this Kiddush may be in doubt.

KIDDUSH AT A BAR MITZVAH

Question: On Shabbat, at a reception subsequent to religious services where a young boy celebrated his bar mitzvah, may the bar mitzvah boy himself recite Kiddush on behalf of those in attendance?

Response: This issue is not as simple as it may appear.

The Rama rules that a young boy is presumed to be a halachic adult upon becoming bar mitzvah at the age of thirteen. This position differs from the ruling of the Beit Yosef, who contends that a young boy may not to be categorized as an adult until he has both attained the age of thirteen and developed at least two pubic hairs (*Orach Chayyim* 55:5). The Rama's position is that once a boy is thirteen years of age there is a presumption that he has developed two such hairs. According to the Mishna Berurah, this presumption is applicable only to laws of a rabbinic nature. Since most boys develop pubic hairs by the age of thirteen, we accept the presumption that the bar mitzvah boy is an adult concerning mitzvot such as prayer which most rabbinic scholars classify as rabbinic in nature.

However, we may not rely on presumptions where scriptural mitzvot are concerned. In that case, it is necessary to assess whether the young boy has developed the hairs in question (*Mishna Berurah,* 55:31). The rationale must be that where Biblical mitzvot are concerned, one does not rely upon presumptions when it is possible to resolve all doubt.

Another way of viewing this is to contend that until the boy has two pubic hairs, his maturity is in doubt. On rabbinic matters, doubtful issues are decided leniently, while on Biblical issues we are stringent on all matters of doubt (*Mishna Berurah* 55:40).

Kriat ha-Torah is a rabbinic ordinance. Accordingly, one may presume that the bar mitzvah boy is a halachic adult and may therefore read the Torah on behalf of the congregation. However, Kiddush on Shabbat is a Biblical mitzvah. Therefore, unless it has been verified that the young bar mitzvah boy has two pubic hairs, the bar mitzvah boy may not to make Kiddush on Friday night for the guests. Comparable logic would apply to the propriety of a bar mitzvah boy reading the Torah on Parashat Zachor which, according to the sages, is a Biblical mitzvah.

FILLING THE KIDDUSH CUP

Question: Must the cup of wine used for Kiddush be filled to the brim?

Response: The Talmud rules as follows: "Rabbi Yochanan said: Whoever says the blessing over a full cup is given a boundless inheritance" (*Berachot* 51a). Therefore, the cup over which the blessing is recited (*kos shel berachah*) should be filled as fully as possible. The implication is that if the cup is not filled to the brim one loses out on the bountiful reward, but has committed no sin. Therefore, if a person makes Kiddush over a very large goblet that contains more than a *revi'it* but is not filled to the top, he has still fulfilled the mitzvah.

This rule may be derived from the following case. The Talmud notes that if a person tastes wine with his finger or with a spoon, the goblet can still be used as a *kos shel berachah*. The Talmud then contends: "The cup must have a certain quantity, and he diminished it!" The implication is that when some of the wine is removed, the goblet no longer contains a *revi'it*. To this the Talmud responds that the cup contains more than what is absolutely needed (*revi'it*) but not enough for two cups (*Berachot* 52a).

At issue is a question that is not even asked. Once some wine has been removed, the cup is no longer full. Therefore, it is not a proper *kos shel berachach* and one should not be allowed to recite a blessing over it. The fact that this concern is not a problem must be because it is not necessary to fill the cup to its full capacity after the fact. One may simply state that a goblet that lacks such a tiny amount is still considered full. Indeed, the Bach presents a lenient rule that in general it is never necessary to fill the *kos shel berachah* to the brim. The principle that a majority is comparable to an entirety (*rubo ke-chulo*) justifies this procedure (*Tur, Orach Chayyim* 472).

The Bach's position may be challenged by the view that *rubo ke-chulo* applies only when one actually has the full amount. That is, a majority is proper as long as one had a proper amount to begin with. For this reason, a *beit din* of two people cannot be valid on the principle of *rubo ke-chulo*. Indeed, based on this concept one must start out with the required minimum quantity, be it a *revi'it*, a *ke-zayit* or a minyan, rather than most of it (*Chatam Sofer, Rubo ke-chulo*, 14).

The Bach's response may be that the Torah did not require a full cup, but only a *revi'it*. Therefore a *revi'it*, and not most of a *revi'it*, must be present. The full cup of wine is not a Biblical or rabbinic ordinance. It is a *siman berachah*. Therefore, even if most of the cup is filled, it still may be considered "full".

HOLDING THE KIDDUSH CUP

Question: Should the goblet of wine used for Kiddush, Havdalah, or any other mitzvah be held in a special way?

Response: Most people simply wrap their hand around the side of the goblet. In this way, they hold it with their fingers, making no contact with the bottom. They simply hold it in the same way that they would hold any glass or cup in order to drink.

Interestingly enough, this procedure is not a universally accepted halachic practice. The Magen Avraham cites the Shelah, who contends that one should rest the goblet upon the palm of one's hand and hold it in place with the fingers (*Orach Chayyim* 186:6). However, the *Shulchan Aruch ha-Rav* notes a preference to place the bottom of the goblet not on one's palm, but rather on one's four extended fingers (*Orach Chayyim* 183:7). Both practices are contrary to common usage. Moreover, the Mishna Berurah cites only the custom of holding the goblet in one's palm (*Orach Chayyim* 183:15), while the *Aruch ha-Shulchan* cites both practices (*Orach Chayyim* 183:5).

I present, for the reader's interest, the following diagram found in an old sefer and forwarded to me by Michael Goldhirsch of Melbourne, Australia. It depicts seven distinctly different ways in which various rabbonim and rebbes held the Kiddush cup.

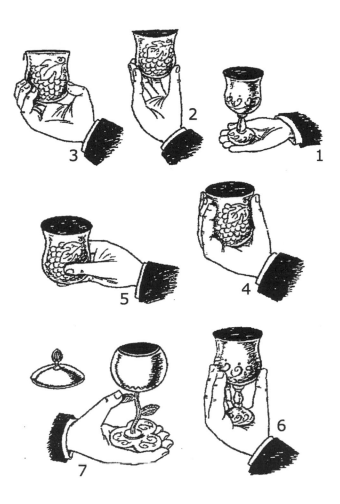

Different Methods of Holding the *Kos shel beracha:*

1. The *Ari* (*z"l*)
2. Baal Shemen Sasson
3. Baal Ayfah Shlomo
4. The Shelah (ha-Kodesh)
5. The Magen Avraham
6. Ha-Tzvi, The Tzaddik of Zhiditsha
7. The Rizhiner Rebbe

(The diagrams are located in *Sefer Pardes ha-Melech*, edited by Chaim Greenfeld, 1929, a collection of customs of the Rizhiner and Sadegora Chassidic dynasties,.)

DRINKING THE KIDDUSH WINE

Question: If one person recites Kiddush on Shabbat for everyone at the table or for everyone in a large room, may those included in the Kiddush drink wine before the person who recited the Kiddush drinks, or must they wait for him to drink first?

Response: There is a general misconception regarding this matter. Many people believe that one may drink no wine until the person who recited the Kiddush has drunk. The *Shulchan Aruch* notes that the requirement to wait until the person who recited the Kiddush drinks applies only when, for example, the guests at the table do not have their own cups of wine and the person who recited Kiddush provides everyone with wine from the *kos shel berachah*. However, if the members of the congregation have their own cups of wine, they may drink regardless of whether the person who recited Kiddush has done so (*Orach Chayyim* 271:16; *Aruch ha-Shulchan*, O.C. 271:41).

There is a slight variation to this rule when one recites *ha-motzi* over the *lechem mishneh*. If one person at the table recites the blessing over two loaves of *challah* and he is the only person who has two loaves, then everyone must eat some *challah* from the *lechem mishneh*. Eating from any other *challah* on the table would not satisfy the requirement to eat from the *lechem mishneh* over which the blessing was recited. Therefore, no one may eat any *challah* until the person who recited *ha-motzi* actually eats of his. If one person has a set of *lechem mishneh* in front of him but another person recited the blessing over a different set, then he may eat from his own *challah* even before the person who recited the blessing starts to eat (*Orach Chayyim* 274:3; *Mishna Berurah* 274:5).

SHABBAT MORNING KIDDUSH: DIVERGENT CUSTOMS

Question: What is the format of the Shabbat morning Kiddush? Namely, what should be recited in order to fulfill the requirement of Kiddush on Shabbat?

Response: Though the Friday night Kiddush is well known, the Shabbat morning version is not as clear cut. In fact, many different customs are widely practiced. The following are the seven most popular:

1. To recite only the blessing over wine (*"borei peri ha-gafen"* and the introductory phrase, *"Savrei, maranan ve-rabanan ve-rabotai"*).

2. To preface the above by chanting the verse *Al ken berach* (Exodus 20:11).

3. To commence with the entire paragraph located in the Ten Commandments that deals with Shabbat and starts with the words *"Zachor et yom ha-Shabbat,"* and concludes with the blessing over wine (Exodus 20:8–11).

4. To recite the above, but to preface it with the verses that begin with the words *"Ve-shamru bnai yisrael et yom ha-Shabbat"* (Exodus 31:16–17).

5. To start with the prophetic phrases in the Book of Isaiah that mention Shabbat: *"Im tashiv mi-Shabbat"* (Isaiah 58:13–14) and then to recite all of the above.

6. To say the verses of *Ve-shamru* (Exodus 31:16–17) and then *Al ken berach* (Exodus 20:11), followed by the *berachah*.

7. To preface the *berachah* (or one or all of the above) with the verses of *Mizmor le-David* (Psalm 23).

Though the first custom is the least popular in terms of common practice, it appears to be the one most supported by halachic sources.

The *Shulchan Aruch* rules that on Shabbat morning, "one recites *borei peri ha-gafen*, which is [called] *Kiddusha rabba* [the great *Kiddush*]" (*Orach Chayyim* 289:1). There are two major reasons for this term. First, the blessing over wine is recited on all occasions at which Kiddush is made, while the other introductory verses are recited only at certain times (Rashi, *Pesachim* 106a). Second, the term is a form of *sagi nahor* – a euphemism in which, out of respect and courtesy, one uses a term that describes the opposite of a given situation. (In this case, the Kiddush is called "great" although it is actually brief.) This Kiddush, which is not of Biblical origin, is rabbinic in nature (Ran).

Both explanations suggest that probably only the bare minimum blessing itself was recited. The Tur *Shulchan Aruch* records that on Shabbat, "one makes Kiddush – meaning *borei peri ha-gafen*" (*Orach Chayyim* 289). The Beit Yosef says that on Shabbat one does not recite Kiddush as one does on Friday night, but "only the blessing of *borei peri ha-gafen*." He also notes that the Talmud (*Pesachim* 106a) substantiates this practice. The implication is that the Talmudic source demonstrates that the Shabbat Kiddush is simply the blessing itself. The Aruch ha-Shulchan lists the first three customs (and adds that of saying the Twenty-third Psalm and yet another practice) and then states that the Talmud supports only the recitation of the blessing over wine (*Orach Chayyim* 289:3).

The Talmud states (*Pesachim* 106a):

> R. Ashi visited Machuza. Said they [the Machuzaeans] to him, "Let the Master recite the great Kiddush for us." They gave him [the cup of wine]: now, he pondered, what is the great Kiddush?

> Let us see, he reasoned, for all blessings [of Kiddush we first say, "Who creates the fruit of the vine." [So] he recited *"borei peri ha-gafen"* and tarried over it. [He paused before drinking it in order to see whether this was deemed sufficient for the Kiddush by day] [Then] he saw an old man bend [his head] and drink.

Thus, the blessing alone was sufficient and no one informed R. Ashi that he had erred. Although R. Ashi knew the format of Kiddush on Shabbat, he did not know whether the term *Kiddush rabbah* indicated that anything besides the blessing was required. The fact that the elderly man drank his wine without hesitation substantiated the custom merely to recite the blessing.

The *Shulchan Aruch ha-Rav* (the Baal ha-Tanya) specifically rules that the reason why the Shabbat Kiddush simply consists of the recitation of the *berachah* over wine is in order to demonstrate that this Kiddush is only a rabbinic obligation (*Orach Chayyim* 289:2). The Aruch ha-Shulchan states that in his youth he witnessed great sages who simply recited the *berachah* for wine to meet the requirement for the Shabbat *Kiddush* (*Orach Chayyim* 289:3). It is also known that this was the custom of Rav Yosef Ber Soloveitchik *z"l.* The custom to preface the *berachah* with various scriptural verses appears to be modeled after the Friday evening Kiddush, which begins with scriptural verses.

The custom that begins the Kiddush with the phrase *Al ken berach* has generated serious halachic debate. The Mishna Berurah, for example, states that this custom is against halacha and should not be practiced. His understanding is that since *Al ken berach* is the latter part of a Biblical verse (the end of Exodus 20:11), reciting it violates the rule against citing partial verses of the Bible (*"kol pasuk de-lo pasak Moshe anan lo paskinin,"* *Orach Chayyim* 289:2).

The Aruch ha-Shulchan discounts this charge. He contends that one may recite a partial verse as long as one has no intention of specifically citing Scripture, but rather to precede a blessing (*borei peri ha-gafen*) with some phrases (*Orach Chayyim* 289:3). According to the Aruch ha-Shulchan's ruling regarding Kiddush on Friday night, however, it appears that he favors citing entire verses even though he does not prohibit the use of verse fragments (*Orach Chayyim* 271:25).

Moreover, the prohibition against citing verse fragments may not pertain to Biblical phrases preceded by an *etnachta* (a cantillation, or trope, symbol that denotes a pause; see Chatam Sofer, Responsa *Orach Chayyim* 10). Since this occurs with the phrase *Al ken berach*, the concerns of the Mishna Berurah may not be applicable.

In addition, Ha-Rav Aaron Walkin contends that the prohibition against citing Scriptural verse fragments applies only during *keriat ha-Torah*, where one may not read only a part of a verse. On other occasions, there should be no hesitation concerning this matter. Otherwise, no person would ever be permitted to cite anything but a complete scriptural verse, either orally or in writing (see Birkat Aaron, *Berachot, Maamar* 108).

STANDING OR SITTING AT HAVDALAH AND KIDDUSH

Question: Should one sit or stand while reciting Havdalah and Kiddush?

Response: There are two traditions. The *Shulchan Aruch* rules that Havdalah should be recited while sitting; the Rama demurs and states that the common custom is to stand (*Orach Chayyim* 296:6).

The Taz notes that one person generally recites Havdalah for the members of the household. Accordingly, the process requires a posture of permanency *(keviut)* that the standing position generally lacks (*Orach Chayyim* 296:5). (The implication is that if a person is reciting Havdalah only for himself, then he need not sit.) However, the Vilna Gaon, who made no such distinction, rules that Havdalah should be chanted while seated (*Orach Chayyim* 296:18).

The Mishna Berurah says that the rationale for the ruling that one who recites Havdala must stand is that the ritual symbolizes providing royalty (the Shabbat Queen) with an escort, and one stands while escorting departing royalty. The fact that people are summoned to gather for the purposes of Havdalah endows the process (according to the view of the *Shulchan Aruch*) with permanency (*Orach Chayyim* 296:26, see *Tosafot Berachot* 43a). The Mishna Berurah notes a preference for sitting not only for the person reciting Havdalah (*Orach Chayyim* 296:26), but also for all assembled who are included in the blessing (*Orach Chayyim* 271:46). (Though the Mishneh Berurah states that one should sit *a priori* – implying that after the fact it is permissible to stand, in his notes [*Shaar ha-Tzion*, ibid.], he contends that according to the Vilna Gaon, it is not clear whether the requirement to sit is essential or only a matter of preference.) However, the *Aruch ha-Shulchan* notes that common custom is to stand (*Orach Chayyim* 296:17).

Interestingly, the *Shulchan Aruch* and the Rama reverse their positions with Kiddush and Havdalah. Concerning Kiddush, the *Shulchan Aruch* rules that *Va-yechulu* is recited while standing, followed by the blessing for wine and Kiddush (*Orach Chayyim* 271:10). The obvious implication is that the entire Kiddush is recited while standing. The Rama adds that while one may stand for Kiddush, it is preferable to be seated (ibid.), just the opposite of his position for Havdalah. The *Aruch ha-Shulchan* notes that the kabbalah was the main source of the custom to stand for Kiddush on Friday night, which was the custom of the Ari *ז"l* (*Orach Chayyim* 271:24). Another reason for standing for Kiddush is that it is a form of testimony that God created the world, and witnesses must stand (ibid.). Since Havdalah has no such concerns, the *Shulchan Aruch* (may have) ruled that one may sit. The Rama discounts the reasons to stand on Friday night but must have held that the mitzvah of escorting the Shabbat Queen overshadows all general concerns to perform mitzvot while seated. As such, he records that everyone should stand.

What is fascinating is that the general public disregards such finely-honed distinctions. Most Jews equate Havdalah with Kiddush. Those who stand for Kiddush usually stand for Havdalah (standing is deemed a sign of great respect). Those who sit for Kiddush often also sit for Havdalah.

SHABBAT KIDDUSH AT SHUL AND AT HOME

Question: On Shabbat after services at the synagogue, a person made Kiddush and ate some cake. When he arrives home for the Shabbat meal, must he recite Kiddush again?

Response: The general rule is that Kiddush must be recited at the place where one eats a meal ("Kiddush be-makom seudah," *Shulchan Aruch, Orach Chayyim* 273:1). The Mishna Berurah cites the Vilna Gaon, who only made Kiddush at the place where he ate his Shabbat meal (see *Bi'ur Halacha* 273 – "Katvu"). This implies that the proper time for the Shabbat Kiddush is just before the Shabbat meal. This is based upon the belief that a "seuda" is a complete meal, not just ingesting a minimum of wine and some cake. Though many people follow the lenient rulings that permit Kiddush as long as it is associated with drinking a minimum amount of wine and eating mezonot, according to the Vilna Gaon's ruling it is preferable to recite Kiddush once again right before the Shabbat meal.

However, Ha-Gaon ha-Rav Shlomo Zalmon Auerbach ז"ל ruled that once a person made Kiddush and ate some mezonot, common custom is not to recite Kiddush again before the Shabbat meal. Therefore, it seems that the general custom is not in accord with the Vilna Gaon (see Stapensky, Nachum, ed. *Ve-aleihu lo yibbol: Rulings and Customs of Ha-Gaon ha-Rav Shlomo Zalmon Auerbach ז"l*, 201:141).

The fact that the Mishna Berurah cites the Vilna Gaon's position without noting those who disagree with it suggests that the Gaon's ruling, that the essential Kiddush should be recited before the regular Shabbat meal at home, may be the preferable mode of behavior. In addition, making Kiddush before the meal permits everyone to drink wine without needing to recite an additional blessing. Moreover, since the Shabbat morning Kiddush consists only of one blessing over wine, its recitation again at the beginning of the meal does not constitute a blessing recited in vain and facilitates the preferred observance of the mitzvah of Kiddush according to the Vilna Gaon.

GRAPE JUICE FOR KIDDUSH

Question: Is it permitted to use grape juice for *Kiddush* on Friday nights as well as for the four cups of wine required for Pesach?

Response: Many years ago, grape juice had a restricted hechsher. Indeed, I recall bottles of grape juice whose labels stated that only "the elderly, ill or minors" were permitted to use it for Kiddush and on Pesach.

Ha-rav ha-Gaon Reb Nissan Telushkin *z"l*, a great *talmid hacham,* Chabad rabbi and the author of halachic books on the laws of *mikveh* set forth the halachic reservations concerning grape juice. He believed that bottled grape juice was qualitatively different from grape juice that had been squeezed from a cluster of grapes. In the latter case, everyone agrees that the grape juice is considered to be wine and that one recites *borei peri ha-gafen* over it. The reason is that such grape juice is still capable of fermenting and becoming wine.

However, bottled juice will never have an alcoholic component. Because of the processing that it has undergone, it will never ferment into wine. This distinction may be so crucial that it may disallow grape juice from being classified as wine for the purposes of observing mitzvot. At issue here is the source for the position that alcohol is an essential element of wine.

The Talmud notes various requirements for the wine that is to be used at the Pesach seder. It cites R. Yehuda's position that "it must possess the taste and appearance of wine." Raba provides R. Yehuda's rationale, for it is written, "Do not look upon the wine when it is red" (Proverbs 23:31).

Rashbam explains R. Yehudah as follows: The verse is saying not to be greedy for wine because of its redness – thus teaching that wine must be red. In addition, says the Rashbam, the red color calls to mind wine's alcoholic content. The verse warns us not to consider the alcoholic component of wine by gazing on its redness (*Pesachim* 108a).

The Maharsha suggests that wine's red color generates alcoholic attributes. The Talmud states that since the destruction of the Beit ha-Mikdash, there is no rejoicing except with wine. As it is written, "Wine gladdens the human heart" (Psalms 106:15; *Pesachim* 109a). A simple interpretation would be that wine makes people happy because it contains alcohol. Therefore, one should not use bottled grape juice, which contains no alcohol, for mitzvot that require wine.

The *Shulchan Aruch* rules that one may use white wine for Kiddush. Though the Ramban is cited as contending that only red wine may be used for Kiddush, the *Shulchan Aruch* specifically notes that the common practice of using wine of any color for Kiddush is contrary to the Ramban's ruling (*Shulchan Aruch, Orach Chayyim* 272:4). It is self-evident that R. Yehudah's citation in Tractate *Pesachim* supports the Ramban's contention. Therefore, some rationale must be provided as to why the *Shulchan Aruch* does not follow R. Yehudah's ruling.

The Vilna Gaon suggests that perhaps R. Yehudah's ruling is simply a matter of preference rather than an essential halachic definition. Also, the fact that the first Tanna does not note R. Yehudah's stipulation indicates that he disagrees with R. Yehudah's requirement that wine must be red. Since the issue is a matter of debate, the *Shulchan Aruch* simply rules like the first Tanna rather than like R. Yehudah (see notes of the Gra, *Orach Chayyim* 272:4).

Since the *Shulchan Aruch* does not require wine to be red, this would suggest that it also does not require that wine contain alcohol. The ruling that wine must contain alcohol is derived from the same rule requiring it to be red. Just as red wine is not deemed to be essential for Kiddush or for the four cups on Pesach, we must also assume that the requirement that it "taste like wine" (in other words, include alcohol) is not a halachic requirement. Therefore, all Jews may use grape juice for Kiddush and for the four cups of wine.

(Interestingly, the Mishna Berurah cites the view that all authorities believe that red wine is preferable le-chat'hila [*Mishna Berurah* 272:10]. Therefore, this would suggest a preference for wine that also contains alcohol.)

KIDDUSH AND *PIRSUM HA-NES*

Question: The Talmud rules that if one has only enough money for either Kiddush (over wine or challah) on Friday night or for lights on Chanukkah, one should buy the Chanukkah lights because it is a special mitzvah to publicize the miracle that the holiday commemorates (*Shabbat* 23b). However, the recitation of Kiddush on Friday night is a means of testifying that God created the world. Therefore, it relates to the miracle of creation which, since it is greater than any other miracle, should take precedence over other miracles, such as that of Chanukkah or the exodus. In this case, should the mitzvah of Shabbat be considered one that Jews must publicize (*pirsum ha-nes*)?

Response: The Avnei Nezer discusses this issue, suggesting at first that the exodus was classified as a mitzvah requiring *pirsum ha-nes* because it took place in public, before the entire Jewish people. However, Creation was by its very nature a private act. For this reason it was never necessary to publicize it. According to the Avnei Nezer, the counter-response to this view is that according to tradition, the purpose of Creation was that Israel receive the Torah at Mount Sinai. This imparts a public nature to Shabbat and to Creation. Yet the lights of Chanukkah still take precedence over Shabbat Kiddush.

This demonstrates that the priority given to Chanukkah over Shabbat has no bearing as to whether it is obliged to be performed publicly. The issue is simply whether the mitzvah is structured as a private or public ritual.

On Pesach there is a special requirement to relate the story of the Exodus to children (Shemot 13:8). Therefore, Pesach is an "other-directed commandment" that requires *pirsum ha-nes*. The Chanukkah lights were originally required to be placed so that anyone who passed by a Jewish home would see their light. Thus, Chanukkah has a public nature. Unlike these customs, there is no obligation to recite Kiddush on Friday night with anyone else present. Therefore, originally Kiddush was never more than a private declaration, even though the miracle of creation was greater than all subsequent miracles (*Responsa Avnei Nezer, Orach Chayyim,* Volume II, Responsum 501).

The Gemara discusses the meaning of the word *"zachor"* (remember) as it pertains to the mitzvah of remembering Amalek (Devarim 25:17). It notes that if Scripture contained only the word *"zachor,"* one would assume that the obligation to remember Amalek was not a vocal obligation but a mental concern. Since the Torah says, *"Al tishkach"* (do not forget) (Devarim 25:19), it is clear that the injunction refers to forgetting by the mind. If so, then the word *"zachor"* must mean that a vocal statement is required (*Megillah* 18a). Thus, *"zachor"* by itself refers solely to a mental, non-vocal act. This suggests that since the mitzvah of Kiddush is derived from the phrase *"Zachor et yom ha-Shabbat"* (remember the Sabbath day) (Shemot 20:8), the prime mitzvah of Kiddush is a personal, private event.

The difficulty with this source is that it indicates that the Friday night Kiddush does not have to be vocalized. In other words, a person may observe the mitzvah of Kiddush merely by thinking it – which, according to the Shagat Aryeh, is contrary to the Halacha. Indeed, the Shagat Aryeh contends that once the Talmud in Tractate *Megillah* finally interprets the word *"zachor"* to be a vocal process, it serves as a general principle throughout the Torah, requiring vocalization wherever the word *"zachor"* appears (*Shagat Aryeh, Hazkarat Mitzrayim,* 12). Nevertheless, it must be noted that the requirement to recite Kiddush aloud does not imply that other people must be present to hear. Kiddush, a personal, private mitzvah, carries no obligation of *pirsum ha-nes.*

PART II

LEIL SHABBAT

EXTENDING SHABBAT SHALOM (GUT SHABBOS) ON FRIDAY BEFORE MINCHA

Question: Is it proper to extend greetings of Shabbat Shalom (Gut Shabbos) on Friday before *Mincha*?

Response: Ha-Gaon ha-Rav Shlomo Zalman Auerbach *z"l* did not favor extending such a greeting before *Mincha*. His rationale was that it is well known that Ha-Gaon ha-Rav Akiva Eiger ruled that a person who said on Friday night "Shabbat Shalom" may, by such a statement, fulfill the basic Biblical mitzvah of Kiddush, which is a requirement to simply remember Shabbat on Shabbat (*zachor et yom ha-Shabbat*). To observe the mitzvah of Kiddush implies that one has accepted the observances of Shabbat upon himself. Therefore, such a person would not be permitted to recite the weekday *Mincha* service; for one may not recite the Kiddush of Shabbat and then contradict it by reciting a weekday prayer. Though it is not assumed that the Halacha follows Ha-Rav Akiva Eiger's rule, at the same time one may not simply assume that his ruling has been rejected. Indeed, the stature of HaRav Akiva Eiger is so great that it is proper to be concerned with his halachic positions. Therefore, it was recommended to greet friends prior to *Mincha* by saying *"a gut erev Shabbos."* It was also recommended to utter the word "erev" softly (*Ve-aleihu lo yibbol*, Vol. I, *Orach Chayyim* 191, 136–137).

Ha-Rav Moshe Sternbuch, without citing a source, notes the reputed view of Ha-Rav Auerbach that it was improper to say either "Gut Shabbos" or "Shabbat Shalom" prior to *Mincha* on Friday because of Ha-Rav Akiva Eiger's ruling that the greeting might prematurely constitute fulfillment of the Biblical mitzva of *"Zachor et yom ha-Shabbat."* Ha-Rav Sternbuch suggests that one need not be concerned with this issue during the daytime on Friday for several reasons. First of all, the greeting of "Gut Shabbos" does not imply that the person is accepting Shabbat at that very moment. It merely means, according to Rav Sternbuch, that one person is wishing another a joyous Shabbat. Also, one certainly does not have intention to observe the Biblical mitzvah of Kiddush by greeting others with "Gut Shabbos," since according to Halacha, the fulfillment of Biblical mitzvot requires conscious intention (*kavannah*) (see *Shulchan Aruch Orach Chayyim* 60:4). He suggests that

Ha-Rav Akiva Eiger's ruling applies only on Friday night after Shabbat has begun. During that time period, the theory is that if one says "Gut Shabbos" after Shabbat has already begun, the greeting may be a form of fulfilling the mitzvah of Shabbat Kiddush. However, before the onset of Shabbat there is no indication that the greeting constitutes acceptance of Shabbat. As a pragmatic custom, Ha-Rav Sternbuch suggests that one refrain from saying "Gut Shabbos" or "Shabbat Shalom" before *Mincha* because one may have the intention that Shabbat has already begun (*Teshuvot ve-hanhagot*, IV:59).

The Mishna Berurah rules that prior to *"pelag ha-mincha"* (an hour and fifteen halachic minutes prior to sunset), the mitzvah of Kiddush does not apply (*Mishna Berurah, Orach Chayyim,* 263:18 and 261:25). Accordingly, before that time it should be permissible to greet others by saying "Shabbat Shalom" or "Gut Shabbos" because since there is no concern with Kiddush at that time, the greeting is no more than a greeting.

LIGHTING THE SHABBAT CANDLES EARLY

Question: How early may one accept Shabbat on Friday?

Response: The Shulchan Aruch explicitly rules that from *"pelag ha-mincha"* onwards one may light the Shabbat candles and accept Shabbat (*Orach Chayyim* 267:2). This period of time designated as *pelag ha-mincha* is considered to be either one hour and fifteen minutes before sunset or one hour and fifteen minutes before tzet ha-kochavim (the first point at which the stars are completely visible in the night sky) (*Mishna Berurah Orach Chayyim* 267:4). The time period of *pelag ha-mincha,* which is not the same for each day, is calculated as follows: the total daylight hours of any given day are divided into twelve equal parts. A day is considered as beginning at *alot ha-shachar* (which is generally assumed to be seventy-two minutes before sunrise) until *tzet ha-kochavim.* This is the position of the *Shulchan Aruch.* Another position is that a day lasts from sunrise to sunset. This is the position of the Vilna Gaon (*Mishna Berurah* 263:19). Thus, if sunset would be at 6:00 PM, then and *pelag ha-mincha* would occur an hour and fifteen minutes earlier, at 4:45 PM.

What is the status of one who accepts Shabbat earlier than *pelag ha-mincha?* The Mishna Berurah rules explicitly that making Shabbat prior to *pelag ha-mincha* is invalid even after the fact (*Mishna Berurah* 263:18, 261:25). It simply is not Shabbat. This means that synagogues cannot use a standardized time throughout the summer to accept Shabbat unless it is reviewed to make sure that services are never held before *pelag ha-mincha.*

Interestingly, the Aruch ha-Shulchan offers a counter-positive ruling. He rules that even prior to *pelag* one may accept Shabbat. His position is that once Shabbat is verbally accepted by an individual it becomes a religious reality.It is comparable to a person who recited the Friday evening Shabbat prayers and then contended that he never wished the status of Shabbat to commence.

His argument is as follows. It is a mitzvah to add to Shabbat. There is no minimum threshold regarding how much time one may add. The Aruch ha-Shulchan suggests that rulings that list *pelag* as the earliest time that one may accept Shabbat may be only precautionary guidelines that indicate a preference, not a categorical statement that one may not accept Shabbat before then. This means that it is allowable after the fact. Thus, one should not protest against those who accept Shabbat even prior to *pelag* (see *Aruch ha-Shulchan, Orach Chayyim* 263:19).

The Aruch ha-Shulchan suggests that it is not correct to accept Shabbat before the earliest time in which one may recite *Mincha*. The gray area is the amount of time available to be added to Shabbat before it begins, but after the onset of *Mincha*. In other words, Shabbat cannot commence prior to the earliest time period allowed to recite Friday's *Mincha* (i.e., not prior to *Mincha Gedola*).

WELCOMING SHABBAT

Question: Why is Shabbat welcomed with song? Also, tradition has it that the kabbalists used to welcome Shabbat with dancing as they sang *Lechah Dodi*. Why did they feel that this was necessary?

Response: The following responses were culled from the writings of Ha-Gaon ha-Rav Yitzchok Hutner, *z"l.*

The Ohr Zarua contends that a Biblical verse serves as the source for the general custom to sing songs at the conclusion of Shabbat *(zemirot* at a *melavah malkah).* The *Chumash* relates that Yaakov did not inform his father-in-law, Lavan, of his desire to depart with his entire family to return to Israel. Indeed, Lavan was so perturbed over this insensitivity that he deemed it an unfair and immoral act. He contended that had he known of Yaakov's intention to depart, he would not have prevented it – on the contrary. As it is written, "Why did you flee so secretly, and steal from me, and did not tell me? I *would have sent you away in joy, with songs, with taberet and with harp"* (Genesis 31:27). From this we learn that it is proper to escort a departing person with song. Accordingly, one should escort the departing Shabbat with song (see *Shelah ha-Kadosh*, Amsterdam Publications, 135).

Rav Hutner adds a nuance of importance. There is a general rule that the joy of departure must not be greater than the honor of welcome. Therefore, *Kabbalat Shabbat*, the service that welcomes Shabbat, must certainly be accompanied with song *(Pachad Yitzhak, Shar u-ve-yom ha-Shabbat, Kuntres Reshimot* 5:8).

Why did the mystics dance in order to welcome Shabbat? The ultimate act of acceptance and commitment *(kabbalat mitzvot)* took place at Mount Sinai. That commitment was more than a verbal statement. It included an action, for the Jews underwent immersion beforehand (see *Yevamot* 46b). This suggests that one form of *hiddur mitzvah* (the beautification of mitzvot) is to associate a commitment with an action. Therefore, *Kabbalat Shabbat* was accompanied by dance *(Pachad Yitzhak, Shar u-ve-yom ha-Shabbat, Kuntres Reshimot* 5:7).

Friday is unique. As the sixth day of creation, it is important in itself. It also serves as the eve of *Shabbat – erev Shabbat –* a day of preparation for the holy day of rest. Because it possesses this unusual role, it requires its own song. *Lechah Dodi* is a song of *erev Shabbat* (*ibid.,* 4:12).

THE PROPER PLACE FOR THE SHELIACH TZIBBUR ON FRIDAY NIGHT

Question: On Friday night, the prayer service is divided into two parts: Kabbalat Shabbat followed by *Maariv,* the evening service, which begins with *Barechu.* The *sheliach tzibbur* leads the *Maariv* service from the *amud,* which is located in the front of the synagogue near the Aron Kodesh, rather than from the *shulchan,* the table where the Torah is read. Where should the *sheliach tzibbur* stand when he leads the Kabbalat Shabbat prayers on Friday night – at the *amud* or at the *shulchan?*

Response: The common custom is that the *sheliach tzibbur* leads the Kabbalat Shabbat services from the *shulchan* and goes to the *amud* in order to recite *barechu* at *Maariv.* Ha-Rav Shmuel Dovid ha-Kohen Munk suggests that this is done in order to demonstrate that the psalms of Kabbalat Shabbat are not obligation but custom (*Kuntres Torat Imecha – Synagogue Customs* 39, note 33).

This suggests that any section of the Friday evening service that is a minhag rather than an essential part of the service may be recited at the *shulchan.* Accordingly, the person (adult or child) who leads the singing of "Yigdal" or "Adon Olam" at the end of the service may stand at the *shulchan.* Indeed, neither of these two songs is an essential part of the evening or morning service.

Another reason why the *sheliach tzibbur* moves from the *shulchan* to the *amud* before *barechu* on Friday night is to show that the onset of Shabbat brings Jews closer to the Torah's ideals. In general, the halachic reason is that Shabbat formally begins upon recitation of Psalm 92, *"Mizmor shir le-yom ha-Shabbat."* This is borne out by the Ashkenazic custom that whenever a festival falls on Shabbat, Psalm 92 is the only one recited. Therefore, the congregation accepts Shabbat upon its conclusion. The *sheliach tzibbur* stands closer to the Aron Kodesh to signify that Shabbat provides Jews with the opportunity to be closer to the Torah. (I gleaned this rationale from a discussion with my father-in-law, Ha-Rav ha-Gaon Rav Yaakov Nayman, *shlita,* the noted disciple of the Brisker Rav).

The specific location within the synagogue where important activities take place has spiritual significance. For example, the honor of being called to the Torah is called an *aliyah,* which means "ascension." This implies that the Torah reading took place upon an elevated platform. Yet whenever the Talmud discussed one who was to lead services, it used the term *yored* (to descend), indicating that in ancient times, it was the custom for the *sheliach tzibbur* to stand in a lower place than the congregants. (This was based on the first verse in Psalms 130, "From the depths I called to You, O God.") This was meant to foster humility in the one who led the prayers for his congregation. Thus, the place where he stood had religious significance.

MIZMOR SHIR LE-YOM HA-SHABBAT (PSALM 92)

Question: Psalm 92 is designated as the psalm of Shabbat. When a festival falls on Shabbat, all the other psalms of the Kabbalat Shabbat service are omitted except for this one. Yet except for the first phrase, which designates it as a song for Shabbat, it contains no reference to Shabbat. It merely acknowledges that it is good to praise God. Since one may praise God throughout the week, how does this psalm relate specifically to Shabbat?

Response: According to Rashi, the psalm is about the World to Come, which will be entirely Shabbat.

Ha-Rav ha-Gaon R. Yaakov Kamenetzky, *z"l,* provided the following analysis. Moshe Rabbenu asked Pharaoh to grant the Jews in Egypt one day of rest each week, which was on Shabbat. At first, Pharaoh granted Moshe's request, feeling that one day of rest per week would increase the Jews' productivity. Upon hearing that Pharaoh would allow them to rest on Shabbat, the Jews expressed their joy by saying, *"Tov le-hodot la-Shem"* – it is good to (have an opportunity to) sing God's praises. Therefore, this psalm was an ancient manifestation of Jewish happiness over Shabbat.

Although Pharaoh later revoked the Jews' day of rest, they lovingly recalled the psalm as their first expression of joy over being granted the freedom to worship on Shabbat (see *Emet le-Yaakov,* Shemot, 259–260).

MAGEN AVOT

Question: On Friday evening, is it necessary for the *sheliach tzibbur* to recite the entire *Magen Avot* prayer aloud?

Response: Yes. The *Mishna Berurah* rules that on Friday evening, when the congregation finishes reciting *Magen Avot*, the *sheliach tzibbur* should recite the entire prayer aloud from the beginning (*Mishna Berurah* 268:22). Even though the congregation already recited *Magen Avot*, the *sheliach tzibbur* is required to repeat it from the beginning.

Magen Avot was originally established as an integral part of the *sheliach tzibbur*'s requirement. In some communities, only the *hazzan* chanted the prayer while the congregation listened. I recall that years ago, at the *minyan* of Yeshiva U'Metivta Rabbenu Chaim Berlin in New York, only the *sheliach tzibbur* recited *Magen Avot*. This was based upon the ruling of the Vilna Gaon – see *Siddur ha-Gra*. However, it became the custom for the congregants to recite the prayer together with the *hazzan*. Since it contains no blessing, the congregation's recital of it caused no halachic problem. However, the custom of the congregation did not affect the fact that the *sheliach tzibbur* had to recite the entire prayer aloud from beginning to end (see *Aruch ha-Shulchan* 268:16–17).

SHABBAT BERESHIT

Question: In some years, Simchat Torah falls on Friday, followed by Shabbat Bereshit. In this case, should the congregation recite the prayers for Kabbalat Shabbat, or should they recite only Psalm 92?

Response: In general, whenever Shabbat falls on a festival, most of the Kabbalat Shabbat prayers, except for Psalm 92, are not recited. This gives credence to the view of the Avodat ha-Kodesh (cited by my grandfather, the Minchat Shabbat [75:5])who had a tradition that everyone must stand when saying this prayer. My feeling is that the requirement to stand signifies that the recitation of Psalm 92 constitutes acceptance of the onset of Shabbat. Just as a witness must stand in a court of Jewish law, one also stands in order to testify to his acceptance of Shabbat. Indeed, the very fact that when Shabbat falls on Yom Tov this prayer is the only official prayer of Kabbalat Shabbat substantiates the position of its essential nature to Shabbat.

The above does not seem to apply when Shabbat falls directly after a festival. In this case, since Shabbat does not impinge upon the festival, the regular prayers of Kabbalat Shabbat should be recited. Yet this is not common practice. A careful reading of the work *Ezrat Torah Luach* by Rav Henkin notes that in a year when Shabbat Bereshit directly follows Yom Tov, only Psalm 92 is recited.

The rationale may be as follows. The general custom is to welcome Shabbat early, even before *tzet ha-kochavim*. Indeed, the *Shulchan Aruch* rules that the custom is to recite the Friday evening prayers even earlier than one usually recites *Maariv* during weekdays (Orach Chayyim 277:2). This means that Shabbat Bereshit actually fell during a festival – and since that was the case, only Psalm 92 was recited. But if one were to welcome Shabbat late at night (after *tzet ha-kochavim*), then perhaps, on a Shabbat that fell directly after a festival, logic would suggest that the congregation recite the entire Kabbalat Shabbat service.

THE CHALLAH COVER

Question: Why must the *challot* be covered during Kiddush? May one use a mesh or transparent covering? Is there any tradition to use only a white covering?

Response: The Taz cites two reasons presented by the Tur for covering the *challot*.

Since Kiddush is recited over wine, one covers the *challot* in order to shield them symbolically from the embarrassment of being present, yet not used for the *berachah*.

The two *challot* symbolize the double portion of manna that came from heaven every Friday when the Israelites were in the wilderness. The manna was covered with dew above and below.

According to the first reason, it would not be necessary to cover the *challot* when Kiddush is recited over *challah*. Yet according to the Taz. the general custom is to cover the *challot* even then, because of the second reason (*Orach Chayyim* 271:9). The Magen Avraham also notes that based upon the first reason, it would be proper to remove the cover directly after the blessing over wine. Yet the custom is not to remove the cover till after the entire Kiddush is recited in order to preserve the proper dignity (*Orach Chayyim* 271:20). The Mishna Berurah cites the Pri Megadim, who rules that the *challot* should be covered until after *Kiddush*. Yet the Chayyei Adam notes that according to the second reason, the *challah* should be covered until after the blessing over bread (*Mishna Berurah, Orach Chayyim* 271:41).

The stringencies of both explanations for covering the *challot* apply at all times. Therefore, we should note the following concerns in addition:

My grandfather, the Minchat Shabbat, suggests that according to the first reason, one should cover the *challot* completely in order to spare them embarrassment. This would exclude any cover that is see-through, since it would not hide the *challot* from view (see *Shiurei Mincha, Minchat Shabbat* 77:8).

According to the second reason, the covering of the *challot* has nothing to do with wine or *Kiddush*. Thus it would appear that the *challot* should also be covered during the third Shabbat meal in the afternoon because *lechem mishneh* is obligatory at this meal (see *Be'er Yaakov, Orach Chayyim* 271:18).

In addition, according to the second reason, a tablecloth or some bottom under the *challot* is always necessary to sustain the symbolism of the manna.

A side issue relates to the color of the *challah* cover. Some scholars (Eliyahu Rabbah) contend that the cover must be white. The Tehilla le-David suggests that the concern may be that it be clean and that no one has eaten with it. The color of the *challah* cover does not seem to be an issue of concern (*Tehilla le-David* 271:12).

FRIDAY NIGHT AND SHABBAT MEALS

Question: If one must choose between making either the Friday night meal or that of Shabbat morning more elaborate, what is the correct choice?

Response: The general Halacha is that the *kevod ha-yom* takes precedence over *kevod ha-laila* (*Pesachim* 105a). The Mishna Berurah explains this as follows: assume that one has a limited amount of delicacies. The principle that the day takes precedence over the night means that it is preferable to serve these items at the Shabbat morning meal. The Yam Shel Shlomo was critical of those who do not follow this rule and nevertheless add extra delicacies to the Friday night meal (*Mishna Berurah, Orach Chayyim* 271:9).

The *Mishna Berurah* presents no opposing view. This suggests that one must make the Shabbat morning meal more elaborate than the Friday night meal.

According to the *Shulchan Aruch* there appears a difficulty in that many religious Jews do not observe this rule. Indeed, the Friday night meals are generally much more elaborate and lavish than the Shabbat morning meals. Accordingly, the *Aruch ha-Shulchan* contends that Halacha does not rule that all food items must be served on Shabbat morning rather than on Friday night. Indeed, the term generally used to describe a situation wherein one has a limited amount of food is *"megadim,"* which, according to the *Aruch ha-Shulchan,* means fruit (as in *peri megadim*). By extension, the word refers to a food item that may be served either at night or during the day with no difference in taste.

Why was this specific item used as an example? Why did our sages not make a general rule that whenever there is not sufficient food for both Friday night and Shabbat, preference is to serve such foods on Shabbat itself? The example may be directing us to a type of food that remains the same whether it is eaten on Friday night or on Shabbat. In this situation, the Shabbat day meal takes preference over the Friday night meal.

However, if there is an advantage to serving the food item on Friday night rather than on Shabbat morning, the Aruch ha-Shulchan rules that it is permissible to eat it on Friday night. He cites as examples eating hot soup and hot fish on Friday night or eating the same items cold on Shabbat. In these cases, there is no question that it is permissible to serve the food items on Friday night rather than on Shabbat morning (*Aruch ha-Shulchan, Orach Chayyim* 271:9).

FISH ON SHABBAT

Question: Why do Jews eat fish on Shabbat?

Response: The custom of eating fish on Shabbat is ancient. It is mentioned in the lyrics of several Shabbat zemirot (see, for example, the stanzas of "Mah Yedidut" and "Yom Zeh Mechubad").

Rav Menachem Mendel of Kotzk suggested the following rationale. We perform mitzvot (kosher slaughter and salting the meat) upon kosher animals before we may eat them. No mitzvah action needs to be performed on fish before we are permitted to eat them. To offset this and associate fish with a specific Mitzvah, it became traditional to eat fish on Shabbat (*Amud ha-Emet*, 72). This may be the reason why some are scrupulous to include fish in all Shabbat meals.

THE PROPER TIME FOR THE HOST TO WASH HIS HANDS PRIOR TO THE SHABBAT MEAL

Question: A custom in many homes is that on Shabbat, the host (or head of the household) is the only one provided with *lechem mishneh* (two *challot*). Everyone present waits for the host to make the blessing over bread so that they can be included in the mitzvah of *lechem mishneh*. Should the head of the household in this instance be the first or the last to wash his hands?

Response: The *Shulchan Aruch* notes that if many people are together at a meal, the most important person should be permitted to wash first as a gesture of respect. However, the *Shulchan Aruch* also cites the custom of Rabbenu Asher (Rosh) to wash last. The *Mishna Berurah* contends that the original custom for the most important person to wash first was common in Talmudic times, when each diner ate at his own small table. Thus, each person ate bread immediately after washing.

In this situation, it was proper for the host or the most important person to be given the honor of washing first. However, in our day when everyone sits together at one table and the host recites the blessing over bread on their behalf, then it is respectful for the host to wash last. This procedure prevents any undue interruption (*hefsek*). The Mishna Berurah concludes that in large gatherings, it is not proper to wait for one person to make the blessing for everyone else because the long wait may cause people to begin talking. He therefore recommends that the most important person wash first and immediately recite the blessing over bread. The assembled guests should each recite the blessing over bread individually after they wash (*Mishna Berurah,* 165:4, 5, 6).

The final recommendation of the *Mishna Berurah* applies to a communal meal that does not require *lechem mishneh*. Indeed, the general custom is for each person to recite his own blessing over bread. However, on Shabbat, the custom of the Rosh has greater validity and necessity. Unless each person is provided with *lechem mishneh,* the assembled guests must wait for the host to make the blessing. Therefore, it is not respectful for the host to wash first and then bide his time silently until everyone else has washed. Indeed, in such a case the host who observes the custom of the Rosh may even help all the guests to wash quickly before he himself washes and recites the blessing.

The *Aruch ha-Shulchan* specifically notes that the Rosh's custom has merit when only the host has *lechem mishneh* and he must include everyone in the mitzvah. Yet the *Aruch ha-Shulchan* concludes that common practice was to have the host or the most important person wash first even though he will then have to wait for everyone else to wash (*Aruch ha-Shulchan* 165:3).

On Shabbat, I have found the custom of the Rosh to be a great asset in bringing everyone to the table in a timely fashion. It is most respectful for everyone to wait for the host, rather than for the host to hope that everyone will wash quickly. This custom is definitely conducive to an orderly process.

(Interestingly, the Aruch ha-Shulchan rules, without any opposing view, that the host can be the only person at the meal who has *lechem mishneh*.)

ZEMIROT SHABBAT

Question: Many *zemirot* of Shabbat contain the Divine Name. May one utter it, or should one use the term *Hashem*?

Response: It is reported in the name of Ha-Rav ha-Gaon Reb Henoch Leibowitz, Rosh ha-Yeshiva of Yeshivat Rabbenu Yisrael Meir ha-Kohen (the Chafetz Chayyim), that it is permitted to pronounce the Divine Name. This permission applies even if the Name is repeated several times throughout the song. The limitation is that in one individual verse, the Divine Name may be sung only once (Responsa *Divrei Chachamim* by Rabbi Aryeh Z. Ginsberg, 91:245). Thus, if the verse is repeated for melodic reasons, the second time it is uttered, one should substitute the term "Hashem."

The Talmud (*Berachot* 6a) suggests that there is a compelling rationale for pronouncing the actual Divine Name. There it is written: "How do you know that even if one man sits and studies the Torah the Divine Presence is with him? It is written, 'In every place where I cause My Name to be mentioned, I will come to you and bless you'" (Exodus 20:21). Commenting on the phrase "I will cause My Name to be mentioned," Rashi says: "When My Name is mentioned for My mitzvot and My words." Rashi thus suggests that God's Name may be articulated during Torah study.

Rav Baruch Epstein, the author of *Torah Temimah*, notes that whoever learns Torah and comes across the Divine Name should pronounce it correctly without substituting the term "Hashem" (*Tosafot Beracha, Parashat Yitro*). His reasoning is that the Talmud specifically states that the verse is a proof text for God's Presence even when only one person learns Torah. The issue must be that pronouncing the Divine Name is the catalyst for eliciting His Presence. It is logical to assume that the Holy Presence descends only upon the mention of the actual Name of God, rather than a substitute term. Perhaps this also occurs when we utter words of praise to God, as in the *zemirot*. God's blessing is a reward for mentioning His Name. Singing praise to God, as is done in the *zemirot*, should serve as a catalyst for Divine reward. This appears to take place only when one utters the actual Divine Name.

This may also provide an understanding of the reason for reciting a blessing before performing a mitzvah. Rashi noted that when one mentions God's Name in connection with mitzvot, the reward of a Divine blessing is assured. When is the Holy Name mentioned in connection with the fulfillment of a mitzvah? The simple answer is that one makes a blessing before performing the mitzvah. The blessing is a springboard for Divine blessing. Therefore, each *berachah* elicits a blessing from God in return.

FRIDAY EVENING ANGELS

Question: The concluding stanza of the song sung on Friday evening, "Shalom Aleichem," is the phrase "Tzetchem le-shalom," a farewell to the angels who, according to tradition, escort Jews home from the synagogue. What is the rationale for the custom asking the angels to leave one's home?

Response: The Torah reports that when the patriarch Yaakov left the land of Israel, he had a dream in which he saw a ladder stretching to the heavens with angels of God going up and down upon it. Rashi contends that the angels climbing up the ladder were those of the Land of Israel, who do not cross its borders. The angels going down were those in charge of lands other than Israel (Genesis 28:12).

When Yaakov seeks to return to his home in the Land of Israel later on, he meets angels once again. Rashi tells us that these angels, who were from the Land of Israel, came to escort Yaakov to the Holy Land (Genesis 32:2). In other words, angels from the Land of Israel crossed its borders. Is this not an apparent contradiction to Rashi's previous comment that angels from the Land of Israel do not cross its borders?

We may reconcile these two traditions as follows. When a person leaves Israel, the angels of Israel do not follow him to the Diaspora. On the other hand, when a person makes aliyah to Israel, the joy is so great that the angels of Israel cross its borders to escort the new immigrant. Therefore, the ability of the angels of Israel to cross its borders depends upon whether they are associated with one leaving or entering the Holy Land.

Just as there seem to be special angels for Israel and different ones for the Diaspora, it may be that there are angels escorting weekday activity and angels for Shabbat. This may be the reason that we sing "Tzetchem le-shalom" on Friday nights. Yet it seems bizarre to ask angels of peace to depart, and indeed, many commentators question doing so. Perhaps we are sending away the weekday angels so that we can welcome the special Shabbat angels as the day of rest begins.

PART III

CONTEMPORARY SOCIAL HALACHIC ISSUES

SERVICES OF A GENTILE ON SHABBAT

Question: Does Halacha provide any acceptable formula for requesting a non-Jew to provide service for or to a Jew on Shabbat?

Response: The *Shulchan Aruch* rules unequivocally that no Jew may ask a Gentile to perform any action on Shabbat that he or she may not perform on that day, even if the request is made before Shabbat (*Orach Chayyim* 307:2).

The Rama adds the principle that one may not even hint to a Gentile regarding this (*Orach Chayyim* 307:2).

This prohibition, which is termed *amira le-akum,* is generally considered to be rabbinic (*Shabbat* 150a), though the Yere'im (113) rules that it is Biblical. Rav Yosef Engel contends that the Yere'im limits the Biblical statute to cases in which the prohibited action involves items owned by a Jew. However, in a case where the Jew requests or "hints to" a Gentile to perform an action with the Gentile's own fire to benefit the Jew, then even the Yere'im agrees that this is deemed rabbinic (Gilyonei ha-Shas, *Shabbat* 150a).

Three major reasons are presented for the prohibition:

Ve-daber davar: On Shabbat a Jew should refrain not only from certain actions but also from speech that constitutes a violation of Shabbat (Rashi, *Avodah Zarah* 15a).

Shelichut: A Gentile who is requested to perform an action becomes the agent of the Jew. Just as a Jew may not violate Shabbat, neither may his agent (Rashi, *Shabbat* 153a).

Sacredness of Shabbat: A Jew may not ask a Gentile to perform actions on Shabbat as a distancing safeguard against Jews performing such actions themselves (Rambam, *Laws of Shabbat* 6:1).

The Avnei Nezer notes that according to the first reason, it would be permitted to ask a Gentile before Shabbat (Responsa, *Orach Chayyim* 43:6). However, even this is prohibited for the other two reasons.

The Rama notes that some authorities maintain that *amira le-akum* is permissible in order to perform a mitzvah (Baal ha-Itur). Based on this concept, "many followed the lenient practice of telling Gentiles to light candles for purposes of a [Shabbat] meal, [or] specifically for a wedding party or circumcision, and no one would protest [such practice]." However, the Rama concludes that since most halachic authorities dispute this premise, one should be stringent except in cases of great need (*Orach Chayyim* 276:2). Thus, the common custom was to use the services of Gentiles on Shabbat in order to perform mitzvot. Though the Rema disagrees with the basis for this practice, he notes that contemporary halachic authorities did not protest against it.

It is difficult to rely on such a theory in modern times for several reasons. The Magen Avraham notes that the reason rabbis did not protest the practice was the principle that it is better for Jews to sin unintentionally than deliberately (*Orach Chayyim* 276:9). The implication is that if those Jews were warned that the practice was forbidden, they would not desist from it. Therefore, it is better for them not to hear from rabbis that it is incorrect.

This should not be the guiding principle of pious Jews. Indeed, if Jews are willing to abide by the rabbis' decisions, the Aruch ha-Shulchan rules that one is obliged to protest the practice. The Aruch ha-Shulchan adds that the overwhelming majority of authorities maintain that *amira le-akum* is prohibited even for purposes of a mitzvah. In addition, he says, "In our day, we have not heard that [anyone] is lenient regarding this" (*Orach Chayyim* 276:14). Accordingly, this law cannot be the basis for its use.

However, some legal loopholes regarding *amira le-akum* have a pragmatic application. The Mishna Berurah rules that on Friday one may merely hint or suggest to a Gentile that some service is required on Shabbat (*Orach Chayyim* 307:10). This means that the prohibition applies only to an outright request from Friday or a hint on Shabbat.

What happens when a Jew asks Gentile A to ask Gentile B to perform a task on his behalf? Since the Jew never directly asked Gentile B to perform the task, there may be no prohibition involved. Indeed, the Ba'er Hetev (*Orach Chayyim* 307:3) cites a rabbinic debate on this issue. Rabbenu Gershon (*Avodat Gershuni*) prohibits such an action, whereas the Chavat Yair contends that it is permissible (see Responsa, *Chavat Yair* 49 and 53). The Shaarei Teshuvah, who notes the Chavat Yair's lenient ruling, cites the Shevut Yaakov (3:22), who agrees with it (*Orach Chayyim* 321:6).

My grandfather, the Minchat Shabbat (90:25), and the Mishna Berurah (307:24) rule that one may rely on the lenient view of the Chavat Yair when great financial loss (*hefsed merubeh*) is involved.

Though the Mishna Berurah contends that whenever the lenient view is followed the Jew should not personally benefit from the *melachah* (307:11), the Pri Megadim, who disagrees, makes no such limitation. He contends, however, that the second Gentile must not be aware that a Jew made the original request (*Mishbezot Zahav* 276:5).

The Shmirat Shabbat ke-Hilchata suggests that perhaps one may rely on the Chavat Yair if the Gentile performs the action for the sake of a mitzvah (chapter 30, n. 48). Yet, the Minchat Shabbat cautions that any matter that is questionable, whether it is a *mitzvah* or not, may not be relied upon to offset *amira la-amira* (*Orach Chayyim* 90:29). The Chatam Sofer rules that the debate concerning the propriety of asking one Gentile to ask a second Gentile to perform an action on Shabbat relates only to an instance in which the Jew asked the first Gentile on Shabbat itself. In a case where the Jew requested Gentile A on Friday to ask Gentile B to perform an action on Shabbat, then it is permitted according to all authorities (Responsa, *Orach Chayyim* 60).

The Biur Halacha (of the Mishna Berurah) cites this view of the Chatam Sofer, yet contends that it is a *Chiddush* (an innovative theory) and is disputed by the Rashba (*Orach Chayyim* 307:2).

Based on the above citations, it would appear that the majority of halachic authorities permit one to ask a Gentile to perform a *melachah* on Shabbat as long as the Jew *hints* on Friday to Gentile A to inform Gentile B of the need to perform a certain action on Shabbat (the purpose is to attend synagogue services and to return to eat a Shabbat meal).

According to the Baal ha-Itur, one may direct a Gentile, even on Shabbat, to facilitate the performance of a mitzvah, even according to the majority who disagree.

According to the Chavat Yair, one may direct Gentile A to tell Gentile B on Shabbat to perform an action, even according to those who disagree.

A word of caution. In a recent conversation with a contemporary Chasidic sage about the pragmatic implementation of many of the principles discussed above (the theories of Chavat Yair, the Chatam Sofer and others), he raised the following objection. The previously cited authorities provide legal lenient rulings for using a Gentile's services only when the need occurs on an *infrequent basis*. The *poskim* decreed that at such times, under certain limited conditions, the action did not constitute a violation of Shabbat. However, this should not be taken as blanket permission to rely upon these principles frequently in order to circumvent the prohibition of *amira la-akum*. The frequent use of such theories should be prohibited, as it is viewed as a contrived way to bypass the prohibition altogether.

This novel and stringent approach does not necessarily agree with general procedures. The Rama (*Orach Chayyim* 307:2) noted that many people had the custom of asking Gentiles to light candles for Shabbat meals. Though the Rama and the vast majority of authorities objected to this practice for many halachic reasons, no reference is made to the issues of infrequent occurrence or regular usage. Accordingly, such a distinction is a personal consideration that some may apply and others may reject with equally good judgment.

INVITATIONS THAT MAY GENERATE SHABBAT VIOLATIONS

Question: Is it proper to invite Jews to a synagogue service or private event on Shabbat if it is likely that they will violate Shabbat in order to attend?

Response: The question here is whether the person extending the invitation is violating Torah law by possibly inducing someone to ride on Shabbat (for example) because of the invitation. This requires a discussion of the concept of *mesit u-madiach.*

Mesit u-madiach is the term used to describe one who incites another to commit *avodah zarah* (idol worship or apostasy) – a capital crime. The Talmud says that in a capital case, the judges of the Sanhedrin put forward the best possible defense for the defendant even if the defendant himself should not offer a viable defense. In other words, the Sanhedrin always puts forth arguments in favor of the defendant's innocence.

Yet according to the Gemara, this rule does not apply to the sin of *mesit u-madiach.* In a case of incitement to *avodah zarah*, the judges do not help with the defense. Accordingly, if the judges should be made aware of a rational defense that could exonerate the defendant yet the defendant does not advance that argument himself, the judges will not intervene by suggesting it.

This rule is noted as being derived from the case of the original serpent (*nachash ha-kadmoni*) who incited Eve to eat the forbidden fruit from the tree of knowledge. The Talmud contends a plea existed that could have exonerated the serpent – when one is commanded by a master or rebbe, whose command is then contravened by a student, logically one should follow the dictates of the master and not those of the disciple. Accordingly, the serpent should have advanced this argument. He should have noted that Adam and Eve were commanded by God not to eat the forbidden fruit. The fact that he, the serpent, intimated otherwise should have had no effect on Eve. Yet the Bible notes that the serpent was punished. This means that neither the serpent nor anyone else used this defense. Why did no one present it? This teaches us that when a person is on trial for the sin of *mesit u-madiach,* they are on their own. Should they fail to provide a good defense, none is brought forth to help their case (*Sanhedrin* 29a).

According to Ha-Gaon ha-Rav Moshe Feinstein *z"l,* the sin of the serpent in the Garden of Eden was not one of apostasy or *avodah zarah.* Rather, it was the sin of eating of fruit that had been prohibited by God. Therefore, it appears difficult to derive from the Biblical incident support for any law relating to *mesit,* which refers exclusively to incitement to commit *avodah zarah.*

Because of this question, Ha-Gaon ha-Rav Moshe Feinstein developed the position that the prohibition against *mesit* is a general sin not limited to cases of *avodah zarah.* Any incitement of another to commit a sin is a violation of Jewish law, regardless of the particular sin. The distinction is that the sin of incitement is punishable by a *beit din* only in cases of *avodah zarah.* However, from a Divine perspective (*min hashamayim*), all incitement to sin, including to violate *Shabbat,* is a transgression. For this reason the Talmud derives the general rule that a *beit din* does not advance a defense for a person accused of the sin of incitement from the Biblical story of the Garden of Eden. Any case in which one incites others to commit a sin is a violation of the Biblical command.

Based upon the above analysis, Ha-Gaon ha-Rav Moshe Feinstein rules that an invitation to attend synagogue on Shabbat that is made to a person who can only attend by driving to *shul* is a classic case of *mesit* and therefore forbidden by Jewish law. However, Rav Moshe Feinstein remarks that if the person has an opportunity to attend without driving, then the prohibition does not apply (see Iggrot Moshe, *Orach Chayyim* 1:99, 159–160).

The basis for this novel halachic approach appears to be the propriety of considering the sin of eating from the forbidden fruit as an example of *mesit.* Should this concern be obviated, then there would be no sources to substantiate the position that any act that incites another to commit any sin is a violation of the Biblical prohibition against *mesit.*

The Margalit ha-Yam (*Sanhedrin* 29a) poses the same question as Ha-Gaon Rav Moshe Feinstein – namely, that the sin in the Garden of Eden should not be classified as a form of *mesit* because it had nothing to do with apostasy. His answer was that in the Garden of Eden, only one Divine command applied. When there is only one mitzvah and that is transgressed, the transgression constitutes a form of *avodah zarah*. Therefore, the sin was classified as a grievous violation of the word of God.

Accordingly, acts that incite others to commit the sin of violating Shabbat, for example, are not comparable to the sin in the Garden of Eden and therefore do not violate the principle of *mesit*. According to the theory of Margalit ha-Yam, *mesit* has no relevance to the propriety of inviting a Jew to a synagogue in a case where in the Jew lives too far away to attend without driving a car and violating Shabbat.

A Biblical View of the Prohibition of *"Lifnei iver lo titen michschol"*

The Torah specifically prohibits inducing another person to sin or contributing to the sin in any way. It is written: *"Lifnei iver lo titen michschol"* (Do not put a stumbling block before a blind person – Leviticus 19:14). According to tradition, the Torah is not referring only to one who is physically blind. Rather, anyone who enables another to sin in any way is also guilty of the sin of *lifnei iver*. Accordingly, the Talmud rules that one who gives a cup of wine to a *nazir,* who may not drink wine, violates this prohibition (*Pesachim* 22b).

Thus, an invitation to a Jew who would drive his car in order to attend an event that takes place on Shabbat should be prohibited as an overt violation of the Biblical law of *lifnei iver.* It should be deemed as if the Jew drove his car in violation of Shabbat at the instigation of the person who extended the invitation.

This prohibition, however, may not apply to the case at hand. The Talmud notes that it is forbidden to extend wine to a *nazir* only in a situation where the *nazir* is separated from the person offering the wine by a body of water (*Avodah Zarah* 6b). In other words, the *nazir* could not acquire the wine by himself. Thus, the prohibition of *lifnei iver* does not apply unless one serves as a causal factor, not as merely a contributing factor. A person who will violate the Shabbat regularly in any case, with or without an invitation to attend a synagogue, is not transgressing Shabbat solely because of the invitation. He drives on that day anyway. Therefore, the invitation is not the cause of the transgression. It is comparable to the case of the *nazir* who had the ability to acquire wine by himself.

A Rabbinic View of the Prohibition of *"Lifnei iver lo titen michschol"*

If the Biblical prohibition is not applicable, what about a rabbinic prohibition? The Talmudic citation (*Avodah Zarah* 6b) notes that where the *nazir* may acquire the wine without the help of another Jew, it does not constitute a violation of the Biblical law of *lifnei iver*. It is likewise permissible, from a rabbinic perspective, to provide him with wine. This shows that in the absence of the Biblical prohibition, no rabbinic injunction applies. Yet Tosafot (*Shabbat* 3a) and Rabbenu Asher (*Shabbat*, ch. 1) rule explicitly that there is a definite rabbinic ban against aiding sinners even when the violation of a Jewish law may occur without the help of another Jew.

In *Shulchan Aruch* (*Yoreh Deah* 151:11) the Rama presents two views:

One may not sell items used for *avodah zarah* to Gentiles only when the Gentile would not be able to acquire them without the Jew's help. If the Gentile can acquire them without the help of the Jew, then it is permissible (Mordechai, *Avodah Zarah,* ch. 1.).

Some (sages) prohibit the sale of such items even if the Gentile may acquire them without a Jew's help.

The Rama notes that while common practice is to be lenient (as in the former position), one who takes higher standards upon himself should be stringent.

The Shach (*Yoreh Deah* 151:6) suggests that the two positions do not conflict with each other because each one relates to a different circumstance. The permissible view related to a Gentile and Jewish *mumar* (a Jew who violates Jewish law deliberately and repeatedly). The stringent position relates to an observant Jew. Just as one must not allow a minor to violate halacha, certainly this is applicable to an observant person.

The Dagul me-Revava (ibid.) hones the Shach's position. Why, he asks, should one not be obliged to save a Jewish *mumar* from committing a sin? He is still a Jew. He contends that the entire concept of requiring one Jew to prevent another from violating halacha relates only when the Jew committing the sin is a *shogeg* – a person who does not realize that he is committing a sin. In this he may be compared to a minor who is not fully aware of his actions Yet concerning a *mezid* – one who wilfully violates Jewish law – a Jew has no obligation to try to prevent such a person from sinning.

Another position is that of the Turei Even. He contends that the rabbinic prohibition applies only when a Jew has a reasonable chance of preventing the sin. In the event the sinner will violate Halacha in any case, then no rabbinic injunction applies (*Avnei Miluim, Chagigah* 13).

Ha-Rav Shlomo Kluger suggests that a rabbinic ban applies when the object that is used to commit the sin is in the control of another Jew. However, when the sinner has control of the object, then the rabbis imposed no ban (*Avodat Avodah, Avodah Zarah* 6b).

In addition, at the moment when the violation of Shabbat takes place, the Jew who extended the invitation is not involved. The Binyan Tziyyon rules that a rabbinic prohibition against serving as a contributory factor to a sin (*mesayea*) is imposed only when the person who enabled, induced, or contributed to the sin is somehow simultaneously involved with the actual violation itself – for example, he gives the *nazir* the wine to drink. However, when the action (or speech) of the person who contributes to the violation has ceased long before the actual sin occurs, the rabbis did not impose any rabbinic prohibition (Responsa *Binyan Tziyyon*, no. 15).

Based upon the above analysis, extending an invitation to a Jew who will most probably drive on Shabbat in order to attend an event may not be prohibited as either a Biblical or rabbinic violation of *lifnei iver*.

The Goal of an Invitation

An invitation to a non-observant Jewish man or woman to attend a synagogue service or a Shabbat meal may be defended as a praiseworthy concern. One may view the synagogue service and/or the Shabbat meal as a means of generating love for Judaism and helping them take the first step in the process of becoming a *baal teshuvah*. In this case, perhaps the rabbis did not consider the invitation prohibited.

A source for this position may be noted in the following interpretation of the Biblical dialogue between Yaakov and his mother Rivkah, who wanted him to disguise himself as his older brother Esau in order to acquire their father Yitzchak's blessing. However, Yaakov feared the idea of deceiving his father. As he told his mother, "Perhaps my father will touch me and find me a deceiver, and I shall bring upon myself a curse, not a blessing" (Genesis 27:12). To this Rivkah responded, "Let your curse be on me, my son. Only obey me" (Genesis 27:13).

The Rebbe, Reb Heshel of Cracow, posed this question: Why was Yaakov so certain that Yitzchak would curse him if his disguise was unsuccessful? Maybe Yitzchak would simply not grant him a blessing in that case. So why does Yaakov fear that his father will curse him?

Reb Heshel answers that the Torah informs us that prior to entering the land of Israel, all the Israelites, in unison, declared: "Cursed be he who makes a blind man wander out of his way" (Deut. 27:18). In other words, the act of misrepresenting oneself to a blind person (in this case, Yitzchak) is deemed worthy of a curse. On the other hand, Rivkah believed that this curseful action (confirmed by her descendants) applied only when the purpose of the misrepresentation was to hinder or harm the blind person. When the goal was to benefit him, no curse applied (see *Chanukkat ha-Torah, Parshat Toledot*). Indeed, history vindicated Rivkah and, by extension, Yaakov.

The same argument may be extended to validate an invitation to a person to attend a synagogue service or a Shabbat meal. Perhaps the sages never imposed a rabbinic ban of *lifnei iver* when the purpose of the invitation was to increase the performance of mitzvot.

It might be preferable for the host or person extending the invitation to prepare a place for the guest to stay so that he will not have to violate Shabbat. Although it is not certain that the guest will accept the invitation to spend the night, the host will thereby free himself of any suspicion of having abetted a violation of Shabbat.

It is apparent from the above analysis that a Jew who wishes to satisfy the dictates of all rabbinic sages regarding Shabbat should refrain from any invitation that may induce even a semblance of a Shabbat violation. However, those who hope to introduce Jews to the observance of mitzvot should be aware that Halacha may well approve of an invitation made for that purpose.

Note: The ruling is based on the view that the ultimate goal is not the Shabbat meal or the synagogue service but the overall and possibly long term Shabbat observance itself. The act of driving a car on Shabbat even to attend a synagogue service is still a prohibited Shabbat action. Accordingly, the purpose of the above discussion was to analyze whether the person who issues the invitation violates halacha, not to in any way condone the violation itself. The sanction for the invitation is merely a first step in the development of a *baal teshuvah*.

A further difficulty is concern over a pattern of regular Shabbat violations. Rabbis have been known to be lenient in individual cases, yet stringent when the violation became a regular pattern. This (stringent) approach is not necessarily the halacha. The Rama (*Orach Chayyim* 307:2) noted that many people had the custom of asking Gentiles to light candles for Shabbat meals. Though the Rama and the majority of authorities objected to this practice for a variety of halachic reasons, they make no reference to the issues of infrequent occurrence or regular usage. Accordingly, the distinction is a personal consideration that some may apply and others may reject with equally good judgment. A rabbinic judgment must therefore be made regarding whether regular violation of Shabbat may be permitted for the purpose of becoming a *baal teshuvah*.

THE LOS ANGELES MIRACLE MILE ERUV

Question: A halachic device, called an *eruv,* exists that can enclose, symbolically, certain parts of a city in order to permit carrying items on Shabbat. May an *eruv* be established in Los Angeles?

Response: Biblical law prohibits the transfer of possessions on Shabbat from a private domain *(reshut ha-yachid)* to a public domain *(reshut ha-rabbim)* or the reverse. An ancient tradition dating to Sinai also prohibits carrying items a distance of four *amot* in a public domain. Rabbinic law extends the prohibition to the transfer of possessions in open courtyards.

From a practical point of view, this precludes the transfer of items from a private home to a public area or vice versa, as well as carrying anything in a public thoroughfare on Shabbat. However, not every so-called public area may be formally designated as a *reshut ha-rabbim.* This classification is restricted to public thoroughfares that meet specific criteria. Indeed, an area that cannot be considered a *reshut ha-rabbim* may be enclosed by an *eruv* (which consists of a minimum of four poles at least ten handbreadths high, connected to each other by wire that has been secured to the top of the poles). This device, which forms a symbolic extension of a private domain, renders permissible, by rabbinic tradition, the transfer of possessions between open public and private areas.

The following analysis is an attempt to determine halachically whether an *eruv* may be established in certain neighborhoods in Los Angeles.

Decisions that affect the sanctioning of an *eruv* are generally accompanied by some controversy, for there are many different opinions on the issue. Some rabbis are ideologically opposed to the establishment of *eruvin* in America. Indeed, sometimes the debate leaves the realm of halachic considerations and enters that of rabbinic politics.

Yet the propriety of establishing an *eruv* in a modern metropolitan center is not unique to Los Angeles. Such European cities as Paris, Warsaw, Vilna, and Vienna all had *eruvin.* So does every major city in Israel. In the United States, many cities and neighborhoods have *eruvin.* Forest Hills, a major

Jewish neighborhood in Queens, New York, has an *eruv*. This area has public roads and subways that lead, via bridges and highways, into the borough of Manhattan. Thousands of people travel through it every day. Thus, the consideration of an *eruv* for several Jewish neighborhoods in Los Angeles is only a Western application of principles and practices that already exist in other areas.

First we must deal with the question of whether the area within the proposed perimeter of an *eruv* contains a public thoroughfare that may be classified as a *reshut ha-rabbim*. Any area so classified invalidates an *eruv*.

The *Shulchan Aruch (Orach Chayyim* 345:7) defines a *reshut ha-rabbim*. It notes in the form of *"yesh omrim"* (some say) that any thoroughfare through which fewer than six hundred thousand people pass each day may not be considered a *reshut ha-rabbim*.

Commenting upon this halachic principle, the Mishna Berurah makes the following observations:

The fact that the *Shulchan Aruch* cites this halachic principle by the heading *"yesh omrim"* implies that the author does not subscribe to this position.

This principle is a minority rabbinical opinion.

It should not be used as the sole basis for disqualifying an area as a *reshut ha-rabbim*.

This principle may be used in conjunction with another factor (*heter*) to disqualify an area as a *reshut ha-rabbim*.

One should not protest against those who rely upon this principle as the sole determining factor for the construction of an *eruv*.

People who are noted for piety should not rely upon this lenient halachic principle to disqualify an area from being categorized as a *reshut ha-rabbim*, but should be stringent only with themselves.

Rabbis who oppose the construction of *eruvin* generally use the authority of the Mishna Berurah as the halachic basis for criticism. Yet it is apparent that the Mishna Berurah specifically notes that one should not protest an *eruv* that is based upon the traffic of fewer than six hundred thousand people. This means that the Mishna Berurah himself would negate public criticism. Therefore, it would be the height of halachic irony to create controversy by using the Mishna Berurah as the source for protest. In addition, it should be noted the Mishna Beurah's decision here is against the accepted mainstream of halacha throughout the world.

The Beit Ephraim, an eminent, authoritative, renowned *posek* (Responsa 26), cites numerous authorities who use the principle of the six hundred thousand as vital to a definition of a *reshut ha-rabbim*. It is noted (contrary to the Mishna Berurah) that the majority of halachic scholars disqualify an area from being classified as a *reshut ha-rabbim* if fewer than six hundred thousand people pass through it. Indeed, this figure of six hundred thousand people is the general rule used by those who, in fact, established *eruvin*.

The Magen Avraham (*Shulchan Aruch* 345:7) states that the majority of *poskim* ascribe to the number six hundred thousand. The Taz (*Shulchan Aruch* 345:7) also notes that it is the majority position and that one should not protest the practice of relying upon this halachic position. The Machatzit ha-Shekel (*Shulchan Aruch* 345:7) contends that the author of the *Shulchan Aruch* does not primarily subscribe to this position and therefore prefaced it by the phrase "some say." However, it is the halacha, for such is the *minhag ha-olam*. In other words, in theory an area may be considered a *reshut ha-rabbim* whether or not six hundred thousand people pass through it. But since the overwhelming practice of rabbinic scholars uses the number six hundred thousand as a criterion for the construction of *eruvin*, this became the halacha.

This halachic practice is expressed by the Baal ha-Tanya in the *Shulchan Aruch ha-Rav,* in which he notes, "Some say that all those areas that do not contain six hundred thousand passing through each day, similar to the Jews in the wilderness, are not a *reshut ha-rabbim.* This theory is the basis for the proliferation of *eruvin* and one should not protest this position, for they rely upon authorities. A pious person, however, should be stringent with himself "[alone]" (*Orach Chayyim* 345:11).

Thus, by using the number six hundred thousand to declare a thoroughfare a *reshut ha-rabbim* is not a matter of practical halachic doubt. Common rabbinic practice has established it as the accepted principle for halachic analysis. However, the practical application of this principle should concern us. How does one count six hundred thousand people? What areas are included in or excluded from this census? Does one include the population only of those who are actually on the street (pedestrians) or add residents who live in homes adjacent to the streets under discussion? Must six hundred thousand people actually pass through the street, or is it enough to have a street that merely has the potential for six hundred thousand travelers?

The Mishna Berurah even questions the necessity of having six hundred thousand people pass through each day. He notes that this qualification has no source in the *Rishonim*. Yet it is apparent that the requirement that six hundred thousand people pass each day is not a halachic innovation of the *Shulchan Aruch*. Both the Rambam and Ran (*Shabbat* 57) cite the Baal ha-Teruma that it is necessary for six hundred thousand people to pass through each day. Also, R. Ovadia Bartinura, in his commentary on the Mishna (*Shabbat,* chap. 11), specifically notes that six hundred thousand people should pass through each day. The *Shulchan Aruch ha-Rav* also notes this requirement without disagreeing.

It appears that the problem is not whether there are sources in *Rishonim* for the requirement for six hundred thousand people to pass along the street each day. This may be noted and verified. The major concern is that Rashi, the primary rabbinic source for this principle, does not specifically note the necessity for six hundred thousand people to travel on the street each day. Indeed, in defining a *reshut ha-rabbim*, Rashi states that it should be *"Ir she-metzuyan bah shishim ribbui,"* a city that six hundred thousand people frequent (*Eruvin* 6a). Thus, a simple explanation of Rashi would be that any city with a population of six hundred thousand would contain a *reshut ha-rabbim*. This means that any large metropolis complex containing at least six hundred thousand people would definitely be a *reshut ha-rabbim* and therefore *eruvin* there could not be constructed.

Rashi's true meaning may be gleaned from several sources. The Talmud (*Eruvin* 6b) states in the name of R. Yochanan that if Jerusalem had no doors that were closed at night, it would be considered a *reshut ha-rabbim*. Commenting upon this citation, Rashi says that Jerusalem has *derisat shishim ribbui* – six hundred thousand travelers (pedestrians). "If the six hundred thousand people included residents, it was not necessary for Rashi to use the phrase *derisat* – travelers. Rashi could merely have stated that Jerusalem has a population of six hundred thousand. Thus, according to Rashi, these six hundred thousand people are travelers on the thoroughfare, not residents. The citation in *Eruvin* 6b merely explains Rashi's position cited in 6a.

Tosafot (*Eruvin* 6a) cites Rashi and also the Behag, who is stated to be in agreement with Rashi. The Behag is cited as requiring *derisat shishim ribbui* – six hundred thousand travelers. Thus, according to Tosafot, the Behag and Rashi are both articulating a similar principle – that the six hundred thousand people are travelers, not residents. This means that Rashi's comment in *Eruvin* 6b is the correct interpretation of Rashi on 6a. (It is amazing that neither the Mishna Berurah nor the *Shaar Zion* commentary notes this citation.)

Tosafot (*Eruvin* 6a) posed an apparent contradiction to Rashi. In *Shabbat* 98a, the Talmud notes that the area under and between the wagons (used for the *mishkan*) was considered a *reshut ha-rabbim*. The area under the wagons certainly did not contain six hundred thousand people. Thus, an area that does not contain that number of people may still be considered a *reshut ha-rabbim*.

Tosafot responds by stating that in the area of the wagons, it was the custom for people at least to come and go. Thus, the question of the Tosafot has meaning only if Rashi maintains that the principle of six hundred thousand people relates to travelers, not residents. Otherwise, there is no basis for the question. The fact that six hundred thousand people do not travel through a given area does not disqualify it from being *reshut ha-rabbim*. Rashi could easily have obviated the question of the Tosafot by contending that access was not an issue because residents were included in the number. Since Tosafot does pose the question, it is logical that the number must refer to pedestrians.

Indeed, the answer to Tosafot provides further clarification and a limitation of the principle. Tosafot states that as long as people generally walk through a certain area, even if six hundred thousand people do not pass a specific physical area, it is still considered a *reshut ha-rabbim* as long as it is connected to a large area on a well-populated street of six hundred thousand people. Although six hundred thousand people are not under the wagons, it is still a *reshut ha-rabbim* as long as people use the general area. This means that while the six hundred thousand people do not actually have to pass through every area or street of the *reshut ha-rabbim,* there still must be access and egress.

Rav Menashe Klein, a modern *posek* (*Mishna Halachot,* vol. 7, Responsum 60), uses this principle as a basis to disqualify any area from being a *reshut ha-*

rabbim where pedestrians are forbidden to walk. He contends that permission to use a thoroughfare freely is essential to the definition of a *reshut ha-rabbim*. Once pedestrians do not have full use of modern thoroughfares, those areas may not be considered *reshut ha-rabbim*.

Rav Klein deduces further (Responsa 60 and 61) from this Tosafot that passengers in cars are not included in the census. Tosafot (*Shabbat* 99a) states that the wagons were deemed a *reshut ha-yachid* (private domain). The area underneath them was a *reshut ha-rabbim* because they were more than ten *tefahim* high. Therefore, what difference does it make whether people pass underneath the wagons? There may have been people on the wagons. Combined with the pedestrians, there were six hundred thousand people in the area. Why shouldn't all passengers on the wagons be included in the census? Indeed, there would be no basis for Tosafot's question.

The answer, says R. Klein, is that once an object is considered a *reshut ha-yachid*, everything in it is not included in the census. Had the wagons been under ten *tefahim* tall, even the area beneath them would have been considered a *reshut ha-yachid*. Passengers in cars, which are certainly in that category, are not to be included in the census. This corroborates the view of the Beit Ephraim, Yeshuot Malko, and Maharsham that passengers in cars are not included in the total of six hundred thousand people who pass along a street (see *Beit Ephraim* 26).

This may, therefore, be the reason why residents in an area are not included in the census. Only those on an open thoroughfare may be counted. Once a person is in a private domain, he has no relationship to a person in a *reshut ha-rabbim*. Each domain has a distinct status. Therefore, a person in a car is in a personal *reshut ha-yachid*. As he travels along the road, the ground beneath the car has the same status as a *reshut ha-yachid*. How, then, may such passengers be included in the census of a *reshut ha-rabbim*?

A source for the method of enumerating the six hundred thousand may be noted from an analysis of the following citation (*Shabbat* 96b): "Moshe gave commandment, and they caused a proclamation to pass through camp" (Exodus 36:6). Now, where was Moshe stationed? In the camp of the Levites, which was public ground, and he said to the Israelites, "Do not carry out and fetch from your private dwellings into public ground." Commenting on the phrase that *machaneh Levi'im* was a *reshut ha-rabbim,* Rashi states, *"She-hayu ha-kol metzuyan etzel Moshe Rabbenu"* – that all were near Moshe Rabbenu.

This quote is somewhat perplexing as it appears to contradict known facts regarding the population of the Jewish community in the wilderness. A simple reading of the Torah (Exodus 38:26) notes that the Israelite camp had a population of 603,550 males from the age of twenty. Including women, children and the elderly, the population of the Israelite camp was, of course, much greater than six hundred thousand. In Numbers 1:47 it is explicitly stated that the tribe of Levi was not included in the census. Indeed, the census of the males from the tribe of Levi (from one month and upwards) was only twenty-two thousand (Numbers 3:39).

Since the vast population lived in the Israelite camp, it appears incredible that it is not categorized as a *reshut ha-rabbim*. The logical response to this problem is that residents are not included in the census. A *reshut ha-rabbim* is assessed only by the number of people who are located along a public thoroughfare. Those in tents or in homes are not included. For this reason, Rashi noted that the Levite camp was a *reshut ha-rabbim* because all Jews were always near Moshe, close to the *mishkan*. This Gemara also teaches us that the figure of six hundred thousand refers to an actual census, not a potential figure. The Levite camp was not considered a *reshut ha-rabbim* because six hundred thousand Jews could potentially travel through it. It was considered a *reshut ha-rabbim* because six hundred thousand people were actually there. This corroborates the halachic decision of the Beit Ephraim (Responsum 26), who requires a thoroughfare actually to have six hundred thousand people passing through it.

In addition, it appears that this Gemara is the source for the Shulchan Aruch, who contends that "Six hundred thousand must pass each day." Rashi does not state that the Jews were near Moshe Rabbenu once a week or at infrequent times. Jews were near him all the time. This implies that they were there seven days a week. The Talmud uses this case to illustrate the principle that carrying anything from a public to a private domain is prohibited by Biblical law. The Gemara even attempts to substantiate the prohibition of carrying by stating that this incident occurred on Shabbat. This means that the incident that gave rise to the requirement for six hundred thousand persons in the area occurred on Shabbat.

On Shabbat, there were six hundred thousand people near Moshe Rabbenu. If a *reshut ha-rabbim* has to be an exact replica of what transpired in the wilderness then it would, perhaps, be necessary for six hundred thousand people to travel through an area on Shabbat. Yet no rabbinic authority has even mentioned such a requirement (to carry out this particular census on Shabbat). From Rashi it is apparent that Jews were simply always there on every day of the week.

If, on the other hand, the requirement is that six hundred thousand people must travel through an area at least once or several times a week (see *Aruch ha-Shulchan*), then the charge leveled against this theory would be that the census should at least be taken on Shabbat to ensure compatibility with the original source.

Some *poskim* suggest that the number six hundred thousand should replicate the situation in the Tabernacle. Rav Shlomo Goren, Chief Rabbi of Israel, has said that the census of six hundred thousand should include only Jews. This theory would restrict the definition of a *reshut ha-rabbim* to eliminate almost any area from being categorized as a public domain. This theory was already advanced by the Eshel Avraham (*Orach Chayyim* 345, Rav Avraham Butchatch) and rejected simply for not having concurring rabbinic authorities. *Poskim* do not note this qualification and as a result, the Eshel Avraham is not relied upon as authoritative.

A modern *rav* who constructed and sanctioned an *eruv* in America is of the opinion that the six hundred thousand must be present at one time. This means that should one conceivably be able to stop time, six hundred thousand people would be present in a given area at the same time. Perhaps the source is Rashi once again. The Levite camp was considered a *reshut ha-rabbim* because all the people were close to Moshe Rabbenu. This means that at a given period of time, six hundred thousand Jews were present in one location.

The Meiri, in his commentary of the first Mishna in Tractate Shabbat, defines the *reshut ha-rabbim* of the Levite camp. He states that everybody went there to ask questions and receive judgment, and *ein mi she-yimheh be-yado* – no one protested their doing so. This would mean that any limitation upon access and/or egress would invalidate an area as a *reshut ha-rabbim*. Thus, accessibility is also derived from the citation in *Shabbat* 96b.

The reliability of this Talmudic citation may possibly be challenged by the following:

Kelal Israel was summoned by means of trumpets. This suggests that they were not always near Moshe Rabbenu. If the entire congregation was always near him, then there would be no need to summon them by the trumpets.

A *reshut ha-rabbim* is always compared to the *diglei midbar*, the banners in the wilderness. But the banners were known to be in the Israelite camp, not the Levite camp.

Perhaps all the streets of both Israelite camps and the Levite camp were together deemed a *reshut ha-rabbim*. The Talmud merely intended to note that Moshe Rabbenu was not in his tent (a *reshut ha-yachid*) but in a public area. Jews were therefore commanded not to transfer gifts from their tents to the public area around Moshe.

These arguments may be refuted. A logical reason may be presented to necessitate trumpets even though everyone remained close to Moshe. *Hatzotzrot* were used to gather the entire congregation. The halacha is that *mitzvot hakhel* (the *mitzvot* that were read aloud when the entire congregation was gathered) included women and small children. This means that when the *hatzotzrot* summoned the congregation to assemble at a given time, women and children were also required to attend. The Meiri (*Shabbat*) contends that people stayed near Moshe Rabbenu for judgment and study. This implies men, who came each day to learn Torah. For this reason, six hundred thousand was the figure presented as necessary for a *reshut ha-rabbim*. It is known that including the elderly, women, children, and the Levites, the Jews numbered more than six hundred thousand. But since only six hundred thousand men visited Moshe, their number became the basis of a *reshut ha-rabbim*.

These six hundred thousand people were probably not near Moshe constantly, but may have come and gone. The *hatzotzrot* were used to gather everyone at a specific time. According to this position, the Jews would have been prohibited from carrying gifts from their tents (*reshut ha-yachid*) to the streets (*reshut ha-rabbim* of the Israelite camp), which was a *reshut ha-rabbim*. Yet Rabbenu Hananel (*Shabbat* 96b) explicitly states that the *gizbarim* (collectors) were located in the Levite camp. If the Israelite camp was a *reshut ha-rabbim*, the Jews would have violated Shabbat the moment they carried an item outside their tents to any of its thoroughfares. Therefore, the simple interpretation was that while the Levite camp was a *reshut ha-rabbim* because everyone was always there, the Israelite camp was not, because residents are not included in the census.

It is not necessarily clear that only the Israelite camp possessed banners or standards (*degalim*). Numbers 2:17 states, "Then the Tent of Meeting, together with the camp of the Levites, shall set forth in the midst of the camps in the order that they encamp. In this way they shall set out, every man in his place, near their standards [*digleihem*]." The Netziv, Ha-Gaon Rav Naftali Zevi Yehuda Berlin of Volozhin, comments on this verse that the Levite camp also had standards, and each household had its own flag. The command was that the Levites should remain close to their own flags, which went with the *Levi'im* who carried the Tent of Meeting. Thus, the phrase *diglei midbar* could easily refer to the Levite camp.

The dimensions of a *reshut ha-rabbim* are derived from *machaneh levi'im* (see *Shulchan Aruch* HaRav, 345:11). Thus, logic mandates that the Levite camp itself was a *reshut ha-rabbim,* regardless of the status of the Israelite camp. Otherwise, it is illogical that specific characteristics of a *reshut ha-rabbim* are derived from an area that was by itself not a classic example of a *reshut ha-rabbim.* Therefore, it appears that the Talmud (Tractate *Shabbat*) provides clear corroboration that the principle of six hundred thousand people does not refer to residents and applies on all days of the week.

Another significant requirement of a *reshut ha-rabbim* is that its streets be *mefulashim mi-sha'ar lesha'ar* – open from gate to gate (*Shulchan Aruch* 345:7). The Magen Avraham (*Shulchan Aruch* 345:7) defines this to mean that the gates are parallel and the street between them runs perpendicular to them. Thus a crooked, winding street cannot be considered a *reshut ha-rabbim.* This rule is the accepted, undisputed halacha.

This means that in order to decide whether a given area is a *reshut ha-rabbim,* one must review its physical contours. Therefore, streets like Wilshire Boulevard in Los Angeles, which have curves, are definitely not a *reshut ha-rabbim.* The *Divrei Malkiel* (4:3) notes that *eruvin* were constructed in large cities even with populations of six hundred thousand because they lacked a *reshut ha-rabbim* that was *mefulash* from end to end. Indeed, he continues, the criterion of *mefulash* is not found in large cities. The *Aruch ha-Shulchan* (345) even contends that a *reshut ha-rabbim* exists only where there is one major artery from the city's entrance to its exit. When one has access to various thoroughfares that lead into and out of the city, then no one street can be deemed a *reshut ha-rabbim*. According to this position, no modern metropolis can be categorized as a *reshut harabbim*.

Based upon the Magen Avraham, it is logical to assume that even the Mishna Berurah would support an *eruv* in a town through which fewer than six hundred thousand people travel, and also whose streets are crooked. The Mishna Berurah merely stated that one should not rely only upon the number six hundred thousand. Thus, coupled with another condition (in this case, that the streets must be straight) even the Mishna Berurah would sanction the *eruv*.

Although the *Shulchan Aruch* (345) states that a *reshut ha-rabbim* must be sixteen *amot* wide, it does not specify its length. However, the *Tur* and the *Shulchan Aruch ha-Rav* note that it must be "sixteen *amot* by sixteen *amot*." This would mean that if a street is sixteen by sixteen *amot* and straight, that area by itself would be a *reshut ha-rabbim*. The extension of the street, which may be crooked, would not. Also, it is possible that if the street had a right angle, then the second part, if it were straight and measured sixteen by sixteen *amot*, would be a second *reshut ha-rabbim*.

Accordingly, each section of the thoroughfare would be assessed by itself. The curved part beyond the sixteen by sixteen *amot* would be considered a *mavoi* – a courtyard that opens to a *reshut ha-rabbim*. However, we must consider this rule together with the general principle requiring six hundred thousand persons. It is physically impossible for this number of people to be in an area of sixteen by sixteen amot no matter which acceptable definition of an *amah* we may use. Therefore, the following options are presented.

The authorities who hold that it is necessary to have six hundred thousand people maintain that a *reshut ha-rabbim* has no prescribed length. However, this implies that if the thoroughfare is crooked at any point, the entire artery could not qualify as a *reshut ha-rabbim*. Those authorities who say that the dimensions of a *reshut ha-rabbim* are sixteen by sixteen *amot* would rule that the census of six hundred thousand people need not fall within the perimeters of the *reshut ha-rabbim* at one time. It is merely necessary for that number to have passed over the area at least once. Thus, it would be improper to count six hundred thousand people over an entire thoroughfare. Instead, it is necessary to assess stretches of a street that are straight and that measure sixteen by sixteen *amot*, and then to determine whether six hundred thousand people actually pass through a given area. To add the number of travelers from one portion of a crooked street to another is a misreading of Halacha. From this analysis, it is evident that Los Angeles does not contain any thoroughfare that may be considered a *reshut ha-rabbim*.

Summary

Based upon the foregoing, an area may be disqualified from being considered a *reshut ha-rabbim* if it lacks one or more of the following:

For the majority of *poskim*, the principle of six hundred thousand people is essential to what areas may constitute a *reshut ha-rabbim*.

Six hundred thousand persons do not travel through any one street seven days a week.

Excluding cars, there is not even a remote possibility that six hundred thousand people will travel there on any given day.

Six hundred thousand people do not travel there (even with cars) at any given time.

Six hundred thousand people are not present in any one place (even with cars).

The major streets are not straight.

Access and egress to streets are limited.

Thus, excluding other considerations (such as overpasses), Los Angeles has no *reshut ha-rabbim*. Indeed, the accepted principle is *Halacha ke-divrei hamekil be-eruvin* – the general halacha is to follow the lenient viewpoint regarding *eruvin*. (See *Eruvin* 46a – Tosafot and Hagaot Ashri – that this principle is applicable even against a majority and even with reference to a Biblical law.)

It seems clear that this is the halacha. Even if one assumes (contrary to my own position) that the matter has yet to be resolved, it is clear that this case is at least in the category of a *safek* – a doubt. This means that it is not certain whether a *reshut ha-rabbim* exists. It is impossible to assert that a definite *reshut ha-rabbim* exists in light of all the authorities and analyses cited above. Since some may hold that it is possible that a *reshut ha-rabbim* exists, together with a possible violation of a Biblical law, it would be at most in the category of a *safek de-oraita*, a case of doubt regarding Biblical law, which is resolved by stringency. This, too, may be demonstrated as inapplicable regarding *eruvin.*

The *kollel* of Tiferet Yerushalayim, Ha-Gaon R. Moshe Feinstein's yeshivah, publishes halachic discourses on modern problems. It is reported that the Rosh Yeshivah himself reviewed the articles before they were published. The following problem was analyzed by Rav David Feinstein (see *Beth Medrash L'Torah v'Horoah,* pamphlet 6, Elul 5736, 30).

A man lived in an area containing an *eruv.* Yet, due to personal c*humrot* (self-imposed stringencies), he did not rely on the *eruv* to carry on Shabbat. On Sukkot, he built his *sukkah* in an area where the only way food could be brought on Shabbat was through a street encircled by an *eruv.* If the man would not carry, he would not be able to eat in his own *sukkah* on Shabbat. The response was that he was permitted to use the *eruv* on Shabbat for purposes of eating in his *sukkah.* The reason given was that an area encircled by an *eruv* falls into the category of a *safek sefekah* (a double doubt). *Safek* means that there is doubt as to whether a *reshut ha-rabbim* exists at all. Even if one assumes that a *reshut ha-rabbim* exists (*safek* 2), there is a possibility that the halacha is that a *reshut ha-rabbim* does not need doors, but may be enclosed by a *tzurat ha-petah* – the encircling of the *eruv.* Although R. David Feinstein notes that if the *heter* disturbs someone, he should carry *(ki-le-achar yad)* in an irregular fashion, he states that the *eruv* is valid according to Halacha. Thus, it is clear that the same argument of *safek sefekah* (double doubt) may be used for additional substantiation for the sanctioning of an *eruv.*

Since thousands of Jews may now be saved from *chillul Shabbat* and many now will have greater *oneg Shabbat,* since the *eruv* is not now being constructed but is up and in order, since halachic practice substantiates the construction of *eruvin,* since halacha disqualifies any area in Los Angeles from being considered as a *reshut ha-rabbim,* since Rav Menashe Klein specifically urged me to sanction the *eruv* it is clear that rabbinic sanctioning of the Los Angeles *eruv* is in the mainstream of halacha and should have the blessings and support of the community.

May the true *posek* and Judge of all bless this decision with *shalom.*

Addendum

It has been suggested that the construction of an *eruv* in some neighborhoods should be curtailed for those who live in other parts of the city because Jews might become confused as to why carrying on Shabbat is permitted in one area while it is forbidden in another. Jews may carry, by mistake, from the section that contains an *eruv* to another that has no *eruv*. Thus, the reasoning goes, in an effort to safeguard Shabbat no *eruv* should be established in any section of the city.

This argument displays ignorance of a basic halacha of *eruvin*. In *Eruvin* 59a, Rashi clarifies the principle of not including an entire city within an *eruv*, even when no thoroughfare within it contains a true *reshut ha-rabbim*. Indeed, the rule is that some area should always be excluded from the *eruv*. The reasons presented are that one should not forget the concept of a *reshut ha-rabbim*, or to note that the *eruv* is the line of demarcation that establishes the perimeters within which one may carry. Thus, not making an *eruv* for an entire city is in conformity with Halacha. Parents have the obligation to train children regarding the halacha of an *eruv*. As children are taught distinctions regarding kashrut, they should also be taught distinctions regarding the *eruv*.

The fact that *eruvin* are not widespread in America also should not be used as an argument against constructing them. *Mikvaot* and yeshivot are not widespread either. Should they be discontinued? The Pri Megadim states that in our times, where a *rav ha-muvhak* is lacking, halachic sources serve as the true rebbe for actions.

No one is compelled to use an *eruv*. It is merely a halachic device for those who wish to use it. Ha-Gaon Rav Moshe Sofer maintains that it is a mitzvah to construct an *eruv* in every Jewish community and that whoever refrains from doing so is categorized as someone who belittles the sanctity of Shabbat (Chatam Sofer, *Orach Chayyim* 69).

Rav Chaim Brisker was known to be lenient toward Jews who claimed weakness or sickness in order to eat on Tisha B'Av. In explaining his position, it is reputed that he said, "I'm not being *mekil* – lenient – but rather *machmir* – stringent – regarding *pikuach nefesh* – saving Jewish lives." An *eruv* is not a *kula*, a leniency regarding carrying, but a *chumrah*, a stringency to safeguard Jews from *chillul Shabbat*.

Following is Rav Ovadia Yosef's Letter regarding the Los Angeles *eruv* (English translation):

> Ovadia Yosef
> Rishon LeZion
> Chief Rabbi of Israel
>
> 19 Av, 5743 (1983), Jerusalem
>
> To our dear, honorable friend,
> scion of a sacred lineage,
> Ha-Rav Ha-g' R. Yaakov Simcha Cohen, Shlita
> Rav, Congregation Shaarei Tefila
> Los Angeles, California
>
> Peace and blessing:
>
> I am responding to the written inquiry regarding the Los Angeles *eruv*. My position is that one may not protest against anyone who wishes to be lenient and to rely on the Los Angeles *eruv*, for those who rely upon it have support. Many great rabbinic sages have ruled on this issue; and some have ruled leniently. However, those who are stringent should be blessed.
>
> Ha-Rav Ovadia Yosef

LIPSTICK ON SHABBAT
(LIMUD ZECHUT LE-NASHIM)

Question: May women wear lipstick on Shabbat?

Response: The normative halachic response is that they may not. Indeed, Ha-Gaon ha-Rav Moshe Feinstein *z"l* explicitly ruled that women may not wear lipstick on Shabbat (*Iggerot Moshe, Orach Chayyim* 1:114).

Yet, although many Orthodox women who observe mitzvot strictly wear lipstick on Shabbat, many rabbinic authorities make no public protest. This suggests a rabbinic tolerance for this practice. One possible reason for it is the belief that if the women are told to stop wearing lipstick on Shabbat, they will not obey. In such an instance silence is preferable, based upon the general principle that it is better to sin unwittingly than deliberately.

The difficulty with this theory is the assumption that many observant women are simply violating Shabbat every week. This negative assumption casts a slur upon the religious character of Modern Orthodox women. Therefore, in an effort to be *melamed zechut* toward Jewish women who wear lipstick on Shabbat, the following analysis is presented.

According to tradition, thirty-nine major categories of work are prohibited on Shabbat. Of these scripturally-derived categories, one is *tzevi'ah* (painting; see *Shabbat* 73a). Thus, from a scriptural perspective, wearing lipstick might be considered painting on Shabbat unless doing so differs in some way from the halachic category of painting.

The Rambam rules that in order to violate the Biblical prohibition against painting on Shabbat, one must cover a space of at least *arba'ah tefahim* (four handbreaths; Rambam, *Hilchot Shabbat* 9: 13).

Ha-Rav Eliezer Yehuda Waldenberg, Chief Dayan, Rabbinical Court of Jerusalem used this argument to permit the use of a thermometer on Shabbat that changes colors when a patient has a fever. He contended that the colors on the thermometer are less than four handbreadths (See Ha-Rav Eliezer Yehuda Waldenberg, "Use of a Digital Contact Thermometer on

Shabbat." In *Pathways in Medicine.* Laniado Hospital: 1995, 61). One may argue similarly that lipstick, when properly applied, certainly does not cover four handbreadths.

Another important consideration is the Rambam's ruling that in order for painting to violate the Biblical laws of Shabbat, it must be lasting (*mitkayyem*; see Rambam, *op. cit.*). At issue is a halachic definition of durability. Concerning the prohibition of tying a knot on Shabbat, Ha-Rav Chayyim Pinchas Scheinberg, Rosh ha-Yeshiva of Yeshivat Torah Ohr in Jerusalem and the Rav of the Mattersdorf neighborhood in Jerusalem ruled, "A permanent knot [on Shabbat] is one that is tied with the intention that it should remain fastened permanently" (The Use of Disposable Diapers and Adhesive Plasters on the Sabbath." In *Pathways in Medicine.* Laniado Hospital: 1995, 44). Since both the prohibition of making a knot and painting have the same condition of durability, it is logical to assume that the Biblical violation of painting applies only if the painter intended that the paint be permanent.

Lipstick is not permanent. Since no woman has the intention or belief that her lipstick will last for more than a few hours, or less than a day, wearing lipstick cannot constitute a violation of the Biblical rule.

The Rambam states that in order to constitute a violation of Shabbat, the coat of paint must cover at least four handbreadths and be permanent. He notes that if these requirements are not met in each case, then the person is *patur* – which means that although he has not violated any Biblical law, he has violated rabbinic law. What happens when both of these requirements are lacking? In such a situation, one might argue that the action was not a violation even of rabbinic law.

There is still another halachic principle that applies to our subject. The Talmud notes that if a person was wearing *shatnez* (a garment of linen and wool, which Scripture forbids), he must cast it off immediately, even if he will be embarrassed. The underlying concept is that where Biblical violations are involved, there is no halachic concern for *kevod ha-beriyot* – in other words, Halacha pays no attention to feelings of shame or discomfort. However, if the proposed violation is merely rabbinic in nature, then concern for *kevod ha-beriyot* takes precedence over the rabbinic statute (*Berachot* 19b).

It is known that many women would never appear in public without lipstick. One woman once informed me that it is embarrassing for her to be seen publicly without lipstick. Accordingly, for many women, the act of wearing lipstick falls within the category of sustaining one's dignity – *kevod ha-beriyot,* Therefore, the concern over dignity takes precedence over the possible rabbinic statute. This means that in this case, helping the women to avoid embarrassment takes precedence over a rabbinic law.

Since wearing lipstick violates no Biblical law (it is neither permanent nor covers four handbreadths) and some women consider it essential to their personal dignity, there are grounds for believing that Halacha does not forbid wearing it on Shabbat. This may also be the correct rationale for the widespread rabbinic tolerance regarding this act.

SHOWERING ON SHABBAT AND YOM TOV

Question: May one shower with hot water on Shabbat and Yom Tov?

Response: Halachic research indicates that bathing is prohibited on Shabbat and Yom Tov regardless of whether a violation of Shabbat or Yom Tov laws took place. The Talmud (*Shabbat* 40a) states:

> At first, people used to wash in [cistern] water that was heated on the eve of Shabbat. Then the bath attendants began to heat the water on Shabbat, maintaining that it was done on the eve of Shabbat. So the [use of] hot water was forbidden, but sweating [a steam bath] was permitted. Yet still they used to bathe in hot water, saying: We are perspiring [taking a steam bath]. So sweating [steam bathing] was forbidden, though the thermal hot springs of Tiberias were permitted. Yet they bathed in water heated by fire, saying: We bathed in the hot springs of Tiberias. So they forbade the hot springs but permitted cold water. But when they saw that this [series of restrictions] could not stand, they permitted the hot springs of Tiberias, while sweating [taking a steam bath] remained as before [prohibited].

Clarifying this rule, the Talmud reports that washing specific parts of one's body, such as one's face and hands, were not included in the prohibition. Indeed, the *Shulchan Aruch* specifically notes that the prohibition is applicable to the bathing of one's entire body, even if this is done limb by limb. Therefore, immersion in a bath of hot water heated even on Friday afternoon would be prohibited because of the rabbinic decree. The codes add that one may not even pour water over one's body (*Orach Chayyim* 326:1). The Aruch ha-Shulchan notes that this latter process was prohibited even though it was not the normal mode of bathing; for once an injunction was set up, he contends, the sages did not make a distinction between the normal modes of bathing and other ones (*lo pelug; Orach Chayyim* 326:2). It is apparent that this relates to showering, which is, in essence, water poured over the body. Today, showering is as popular a mode of bathing as immersing oneself in a bathtub.

One cannot contend that the original prohibition did not include showering because it was not a conventional mode of bathing at the time.

Indeed, the Talmud specifically states that bathing in the hot springs of Tiberias was made permissible, because without such permission the Jews would have had no acceptable means of bathing with hot water on Shabbat (see Rashi). This indicates that hot showers was also prohibited. Accordingly, any form of bathing with hot water, even with hot water heated prior to Shabbat or without any violation of Shabbat (such as an automatic heater) would be prohibited. (My own feeling is that the decree would extend to immersing one's entire body in a heated swimming pool.)

However, Ha-Rav Akiva Eiger provides a loophole. He contends that a person who is in pain may bathe on Shabbat even if he is not ill. Therefore, the decree did not apply to a person who would feel pain or anguish if he did not bathe. Such a person may use hot water with no violation of Shabbat (Glosses, Rav Akiva Eiger, *Orach Chayyim* 326:1).

Concerning Yom Tov, the Talmud records an incident in which bathing with water heated on Erev Yom Tov was prohibited (see also Tosafot: *Le-motzei*). Indeed, based upon the Talmud itself, without further research or analysis, a general approach was to assume that showering or bathing with hot water on Yom Tov was prohibited because of the rabbinic decree. Yet what is the reason for this prohibition?

On Shabbat, it is forbidden to heat water. Therefore, the use of hot water, even if it was heated before Shabbat, was prohibited in order to prevent heating water on Shabbat itself. However, on Yom Tov we may heat water for drinking or cooking purposes. In addition, there is a rule that states that when an item is permitted for purposes of food, it is also permitted for non-food purposes (*mi-toch*). By this logic, since one may heat water for a meal, it should also be permissible to heat water for a bath.

Here are two responses to the above. 1. Rabbenu Asher, citing the Riva, contends that on Yom Tov one may only perform those activities that most people practice (*shaveh la-kol*). However, if a given activity is performed only by a small group of people, it is prohibited even on Yom Tov (Rosh, *Shabbat,* Chapter 1).

First, according to the Rosh, only very sensitive people were accustomed to bathing their entire bodies every day, while the daily bathing of limbs (such as the head, face and legs) was common practice. Second, the Aruch ha-Shulchan notes that the Rambam does not list the above theory. According to the Rambam, bathing with hot water on Yom Tov is prohibited because of the fear of violating Shabbat laws. Yom Tov was simply included in the ban (495:19).

There are serious questions as to whether the first theory applies in our day. The Shmirat Shabbat ke-Hilchata notes that today, almost all people have private bathrooms and daily bathing is common. Since it is no longer reserved for the wealthy or the extremely sensitive, it should be permitted on Yom Tov.

Also, it is permissible to heat water on Yom Tov in order to wash one's head. If that action is permissible, then one may also bathe in the same hot water, because the faucet that one opens in order to wash one's head uses the same process that runs a bath or shower. It also may be possible to challenge the Rambam's position somewhat because it is not customary to forbid an activity on Yom Tov because of a possible violation of Shabbat. (The response to this is it may have been forbidden on Yom Tov because of the prohibition of *sechita* – wringing or squeezing – on that day.)

It is still customary that many religious Jews who smoke do so on Yom Tov. Although smoking is certainly not the general custom, the rabbinic world does not protest against those who smoke on Yom Tov. The halachic position of the smokers is that it is necessary for them to smoke even on Yom Tov. This rationale should also apply to the people who bathe every day. It is necessary to feel clean (*Shmirat Shabbat ke-Hilchata,* Chapter 14:7, n. 21).

Therefore, a person who seeks to bathe with hot water on Yom Tov should be directed to shower, since showering appears to be somewhat different from the type of bathing covered by the original rabbinic decree. Also, if the person has perspired a great deal and is in great discomfort or pain, this supersedes the decree, according to R. Akiva Eiger.

(The above discussion does not apply to a *mikveh* that is used for the performance of a mitzvah. The use of warm or hot *mikva'ot* is a separate issue. Also, contrary to previous generations, many current Rabbis prohibit smoking as dangerous to health and, therefore, also prohibited on Yom Tov.)

PLAYING BALL ON SHABBAT AND YOM TOV

Question: Is it permitted to play ball on Shabbat and Yom Tov?

Response: The proliferation of *eruvin* throughout North America has allowed observant Jews the freedom to carry in public areas on Shabbat, an activity that had hitherto been forbidden. However, this license generated the impression that within the perimeters of the *eruv*, any activity that involves carrying is permitted, including playing ball. Concomitantly, as Jews frequent an ever-expanding number of kosher resorts, it is assumed that there are no limits on usage of hotel facilities on Shabbat and Yom Tov, including that of tennis courts. Of concern is the halachic propriety of such activities on Shabbat and/or Yom Tov.

The *Shulchan Aruch* rules, "It is forbidden to play ball on Shabbat and Yom Tov." The Rama notes, "Some permit it, and the common custom is to be lenient" (*Orach Chayyim* 308:45). Since the Rama does not qualify his permissive ruling, it appears applicable to everyone regardless of gender, age or location. Thus, while playing ball on Shabbat and Yom Tov may not be considered an expression of the spiritual joy of those days, nevertheless it may be a halachically acceptable activity for those who enjoy it. It is a means of *oneg* on Shabbat and Yom Tov. Indeed, *Tosafot* explicitly rules that one may play ball on Yom Tov (*Tos. Betzah* 12a).

A review of halachic authorities, however, indicates that the issue is not so clear-cut and that a more restrictive approach may be in order.

Rav Shlomo Luria (the Rashal) criticizes the blanket permission to play ball on Yom Tov. He notes that playing ball has no normal function or purpose on that day. It was tolerable "only for young children who did not fall within the age of obligation." As for "adults, it is bad practice, a form of levity." He suggests that if he had the authority, he would have "abolished ball-playing on Yom Tov altogether" (*Yam shel Shlomo, Betza* 1:34). According to this line of reasoning, ball-playing should be forbidden on Shabbat as well, even within a private building or inside an *eruv*.

Later *Acharonim* relied upon Rashal's statements to modify those of the Rama. *Magen Avraham* (*Orach Chayyim* 518:4) and *Taz* (*Orach Chayyim* 518:2) both cite Rashal's opinion and rule that ball-playing is permitted only to minors. The *Mishna Berurah* also cites Rashal, adding that playing ball on Yom Tov is not clearly as permissible as commonly believed, since *the Shulchan Aruch* clearly prohibits it (*Orach Chayyim* 518:9). Thus, the *Mishna Berurah* notes to imply that since the status of ball playing on Shabbat and Yom Tov is a matter of contention between *Shulchan Aruch* and *Rama*, those who accept the lenient view should at the very least follow the Rashal's ruling that that leniency is for minors only.

Magen Avraham cites Aharonim who contend that those who allow ball playing do so only on Yom Tov and not on Shabbat (*Magen Avraham, Orach Chayyim* 308:73). However, *Aruch ha-Shulchan* rejects any distinction between Shabbat and Yom Tov on this question (*ibid.,* 308:70). The position of *Magen Avraham* may be rooted in a distinction between Shabbat and Yom Tov.

Unlike Shabbat, the observance of Yom Tov contains room for personal enjoyment, each according to his preference (*hatzi lachem*). Therefore, it may be said that even those authorities who permit ball-playing on Yom Tov can forbid it on Shabbat. If ball playing were allowed on Shabbat, it would be allowed *a fortiori* on Yom Tov (see *Betza* 15b and *Shulchan Aruch, Orach Chayyim* 529:1).

Aruch ha-Shulchan responded to Rashal's argument by noting that as long as some people enjoy playing ball, even if they are not of high level spiritual character (*da'ato ha-shefela*), they should not be forbidden to do so (*Orach Chayyim* 518:8). *Aruch ha-Shulchan* may reflect the opinion of *Terumat ha-Deshen* (no. 61), that *oneg Shabbat* contains a subjective element. Still, the practical result of his words is unclear. On the one hand, one might deduce that ball playing is allowed. On the other, some see in the *Aruch ha-Shulchan*'s words only a justification for current practice that would be forbidden under other circumstances (R. Yitzchak Yosef, *Sefer Yalkut Yosef* IV, 388–389). In any event, we should strive to elevate the expression of the sanctity of Shabbat and Yom Tov, and not to cater to those "of simpler mind/spirit."

It is suggested that the fact that Rashal allows limited ball playing, i.e., for children, means that the ball itself cannot be considered *muktzeh*. Therefore, the concern of Rama and Rashal is with ball playing rather than with the ball itself. The result is that when ball playing is allowed, as when young children play, the ball may not be considered *muktzeh* even for an adult. This is in contradistinction to the view of Rav Yosef Chaim Sonnenfeld that ball-playing is forbidden even to soothe a crying child (*Resp. Salmat Chayyim* 1:71).

His opinion, however, is based upon his advocacy of the position of *Beit Yosef,* who considers the ball *muktzeh.* Those of us who accept the position of Rama as modified by Rashal could allow this as well.

A careful reading of Rashal's formulation shows that he did not allow all minors to play ball on Yom Tov either. It should be recalled that Rashal tolerated the activity "only for young children who did not fall within the age of obligation." It is reasonable to interpret the "age of obligation" as being the age of *chinuch* – education. The exact age of *chinuch* is a matter of some disagreement among *Rishonim* (see the summary in *Encyclopedia Talmudit*, vol. 16, Jerusalem: 1980, 167–169). What is clear, however, is after bar or bat mitzvah age, a child is no longer a minor. This means that rabbis and yeshivah educators should make it clear to young people that playing ball after bar/bat mitzvah is not an acceptable activity on Shabbat or Yom Tov. Accordingly, *fortiori*, ball-playing by adults on such occasions is definitely improper.

Indeed, even minors who play ball on Shabbat or Yom Tov must be taught to do so discreetly (such as in back yards) and not to make it a public event. Careful attention should also be paid to the type of playing field upon which the games are played. Rama, for example, rules that playing with nuts on an earthen floor is prohibited out of concern that one might "smooth holes" (*masveh gumot*). Hence, ball playing on non-paved or non-seeded ground is forbidden (Orach Chayyim 385:5 and *Mishna Berurah*, 308:158). R. Na'eh notes in his discussion, even those authorities who permit ball playing do so only on an *ad hoc* basis, but certainly not as a scheduled event (*Badei ha-Shulchan, ibid.*).

It is recorded that the city of Tur Shimon was destroyed because its inhabitants played ball on Shabbat (*Yerushalmi Ta'anit* 4:5). *Mateh Moshe* contends that the inhabitants of Tur Shimon sinned by playing ball at a time set aside for Torah study. Ball-playing thus became a cause of *bittul Torah* on Shabbat and Yom Tov. Accordingly, he writes, it is obvious "that ball-playing when no *shiur* was occurring would be permitted. This, too, is the reported position of *Tosafot* in *Betza* that one may play ball on Shabbat and Yom Tov" (R. Moshe Mat, *Sefer Mateh Moshe,* Jerusalem, 1982, sec. 477. In our text, Tosafot does not mention Shabbat). In other words, Tosafot would have forbidden ball-playing during public Torah lectures and classes. Thus, playing ball was prohibited not because it detracted from the sanctity of

Shabbat but because it lured Jews away from Torah learning. This indicates that even Tosafot never granted blanket permission to play ball.

The theory of *Mateh Moshe* requires further thought. Was Tur Shimon destroyed just because ball-playing took place at the same time as actual public shiurim? If so, the problem could have been solved by revising schedules. However, it is suggested that Mateh Moshe's position is that ball-playing is prohibited on Shabbat and Yom Tov whenever public shiurim *could* be held.

Mateh Moshe notes that common custom was not to study the Oral Law publicly after *Mincha* on Shabbat because tradition had it that Moshe Rabbenu passed away at that time, and the rule is that when a great scholar dies, all *batei midrash* are closed in his honor (*ibid.*, sec. 485). Thus, according to Mateh Moshe, ball-playing would be allowed after *Mincha* on Shabbat.

Not all authorities accept this interpretation of Mateh Moshe. According to another *midrash* cited by the Rosh, Moshe Rabbenu wrote or finished thirteen Torah scrolls on the day of his death. One was given to each of the twelve tribes and the last was placed in the Ark of the Covenant (*Midrash, Devarim Rabbah, Parshat Va-yelech*, sec. 9). The Rosh argues that this tradition refutes the contention that Moshe died on Shabbat, for if he did, how could he have written the Torah Scrolls? Therefore, he concludes, there is no basis for the custom of abstaining from study between *Mincha* and *Maariv* on Shabbat afternoon (*Rosh, Pesachim* 10:3). Should one accept this view of the Rosh – that Torah study is permitted throughout Shabbat – then ball-playing would be prohibited throughout the day. Accordingly, on Yom Tov, it would also always be forbidden to play ball. Thus, Mateh Moshe's position is at variance with that of Tosafot, who explicitly allowed ball-playing on Yom Tov.

Rashal may have been disturbed by the conflict between the tradition regarding Tur Shimon and the common custom of playing ball on holidays. Rashal may be seen to have harmonized the two positions by noting that ball-playing serves no purpose on Yom Tov. It is an activity for children, not adults. In addition, Rashal states that ball-playing is not "comparable to carrying a minor child; for in the latter instance the father is happy and derives pleasure from his child, and this can be termed *simchat yom tov*" (*Yam Shal Shlomo, Betza* 1:34). In other words, an activity with a minor child is permitted, while ball-playing is forbidden. Yet why should the joy of playing ball with adults be less than that of playing with children? In addition, Rashal rules that if an *eruv* exists, one may carry from one courtyard to another even items which may have no purpose on Yom Tov. This contradicts his ruling about balls and ball playing. Why could Rashal not have extended permission to the latter within the confines of an *eruv*?

The answer appears to be that the basis for the prohibition on playing ball was the traumatic reaction to the destruction of Tur Shimon, which caused the sages to ban all ball-playing by adults on Shabbat and Yom Tov. They did not wish holy days to be given over to ball games instead of spiritual matters. This is Rashal's unique position. Apart from the above reactions to the destruction of Tur Shimon, a number of interpretations may be offered. One might even contend that the rabbis prohibited only ball-playing, which took place throughout most of Yom Tov and Shabbat. Accordingly, if a person goes to the synagogue for communal prayer and attends public Torah lessons, then, perhaps, ball-playing would also be permitted. Yet the sages do not even mention such a position. In addition, since Rashal's position was accepted by the majority of poskim, it appears that his interpretation of the reaction to Tur Shimon is normative.

Taz *(Orach Chayyim 518, p. 1)*, *Magen Avraham (ibid., p. 4)* and *Mishna Berurah* (Orach Chayyim 518:12) cite Rashal as forbidding adults to play ball on Shabbat and on Yom Tov and make no exception when an *eruv* is present. The obvious implication is that Rashal's position applies even within the confines of an *eruv*.

Conclusion

The organization of and participation in a ball game for children above the age of *chinuch* may be a violation of the Torah's injunction that Shabbat and Yom Tov be "sacred assemblies" (*mikra'ei kodesh*). As expressed by Ramban in his commentary on the Torah, this mitzvah teaches that Shabbat and Yom Tov must be distinguished from the rest of the week by the modes of dress, eating and each individual's general deportment. In this way, one's total ambience will be conducive to the creation of a day sacred to God (*Leviticus* 23:2). Sforno notes that the meaning of *mikra'ei kodesh* is that Shabbat should be devoted to assemblage for purposes of *kedushah (ibid.)*.

Another area of Shabbat *halacha* that is germane here is the Torah's command, "On the seventh day you shall rest" (Exodus 23:12 and Rashi's commentary; the fullest exposition of this idea may be found in Ramban's commentary on Leviticus 23:24). Organized ball games may be a violation of this mitzvah (*Cf.* Ramban, *Drasha le-Rosh ha-Shanah, Kitvei Ramban* II, 217–219. See also Orach Chayyim 328:42 and *Mishna Berurah, ibid.*).

Finally, it is apparent that ball playing and similar activities may constitute a violation (*bittul aseh*) of the Torah's command that we "Remember the Sabbath day to make it holy" (Exodus 20:8). Ramban explains that the Torah's intent here is to teach us to refrain from preoccupation with worldly matters and to give ourselves spiritual pleasure in the ways of God through the active cultivation of activities that are conducive to it (*ibid.;* see also the comments of Sforno, *ad loc.*).

The conclusion that we may derive from the above is clear. Our communities should follow the halacha that has been stated by most codifiers, including *Mishna Berurah.* Rabbis, as the authorities responsible for the spiritual welfare of their communities, should unite with parents and educators to assume responsibility and ensure that our children learn to respect the special spirit of Shabbat and Yom Tov. The following recommendations should be made:

Organized ball games (or other athletic activities) that involve anyone over the age of bar/bat mitzvah appear to be in violation of *uvda de-chol.* They contravene the mitzvot of *mikra'ei kodesh* and *ba-yom ha-shevi'i tishbot.* Thus, they should be strongly discouraged (See *Shemirat Shabbat ke-Hilchata* 16:1).

While most Ashkenazic authorities permit children under the age of five to play ball, most Sephardic halachists accept the view that a ball is *muktzeh* and therefore forbid it (*Cf. Yalkut Yosef, ibid.,* 387–391). However, R. Chayyim David Ha-Levi, the Sephardi Chief Rabbi of Tel Aviv, contends that a careful reading of the *Shibbolei ha-Leket* suggests that the issue relating to ball-playing is not one of *muktzeh,* but rather a concern for *kavod* and *zilzul Shabbat* (*Aseh Lecha Rav* 11, Jerusalem, 94–96).

Between the ages of five (commonly assumed to be the lowest age for *chinuch*), and bar/bat mitzvah, the propriety of ball-playing may be a matter of dispute due to a difference of opinion regarding the age of *chinuch.* Therefore its appropriateness will depend upon the evaluation of the rabbi of the individual children involved and the community's requirements. See the discussion in *Shemirat Shabbat ke-Hilchata,* 163, n. 11, that according to R.

Shlomo Zalman Auerbach, banging stones with a child below the age of chinuch in order to pacify him/her is permitted. Other authorities permit this when done in an unusual fashion, i.e., *ki-le-achar yad*. Under these circumstances, according to R. Auerbach, the rocks would not be considered *muktzeh*. It is reasonable, therefore, to conclude that playing ball with a child of this age would be permitted, certainly if it is done *ki-le-achar yad*.

Alternate forms of activity should be designed to occupy, educate and entertain children in keeping with the atmosphere of Shabbat.

The sanctity of Shabbat warrants special precautions and considerations. The Orthodox community must rise to the occasion to protect this holy day.

A Dishwasher with a Timer on Shabbat

Question: If one has a dishwasher that operates on a time clock, may the dishwasher be programmed to operate by itself on Shabbat or Yom Tov as long as the programming is done beforehand?

Response: Ha-Rav ha-Gaon Moshe Feinstein, *z"l*, prohibits such usage for Shabbat. However, he permits the use of a time clock to turn electric lights on and off on Shabbat. Yet, he openly warns that one may not deduce from this ruling that other Melachot of Shabbat are also permitted if they are programmed in advance with a timer. Indeed, he specifically prohibits the use of a timer for any activity other than turning lights on and off. He does, moreover, even note that this prohibition is operational even though there does not appear to be any logical reason for permitting a timer for electric lights and prohibiting a timer for other Melaclhot of Shabbat, such as cooking food (see *Iggrot Moshe, Orach Chayyim,* 5:22:5, and also *Iggrot Moshe* 4:60).

The difficulty with this ruling is that logically, the legal loophole of the time clock for lights should not be restricted to turning lights on and off. It should be used to permit a variety of Shabbat *melachot.* In other words, all actions that have been prepared before Shabbat should be permitted on Shabbat because there is no halachic prohibition against machinery, without any Jewish or human input, working automatically on Shabbat.

The fact that Rav Moshe Feinstein does not use this loophole indicates that there may be other reasons for the permission to use a timer for lights. Rav Moshe Feinstein notes that in Europe it was common to permit using the services of Gentiles to turn lights on and off on Shabbat. Therefore, the very fact that lights go on or off on Shabbat would not be unusual or startling. Since there is a well-established custom to permit the kindling or extinguishing of lights in some way, one may rely on the Shabbat timer to turn lights on and off. In other activities, however, the fact that the machinery goes on and off may cause a decrease in respect for Shabbat *(ziluta de-Shabbat).* (See *Iggrot Moshe, Orach Chayyim* 4:60). In other words, concern for reactions to machinery operated by a timer appears to be basic to Rav Feinstein's reluctance to allow the use of a timer for activities other than lights.

Not every authority agrees. Ha-Rav ha-Gaon Rav Shlomo Zalman Auerbach *z"l* ruled that one may use a dishwasher on Shabbat that was programmed by a timer on erev Shabbat to go on and off automatically. However, he ruled against its use when there was a concern over noise, which might lower respect for Shabbat. Yet the basic ruling is that the use of a timer for a dishwasher on Shabbat is allowed as long as people are aware that it was programmed before Shabbat (see *Ve-aleihu lo yibol* 187, pages 134 and 135).

It appears that Rav Auerbach's ruling is based on the general principle deduced from the ruling that permits the use of a Shabbat clock to turn lights on and off on Shabbat. To offset the concern of *ashva milta* (noise) or apprehensions that the activity seems to be not proper for Shabbat *(uvdin de-chol)*, it is suggested that the dishwasher operate in the middle of the night when no one is about. This is based on the ruling of the Maharsham, Ha-Rav ha-Gaon Rav Sholom Mordechai Schwadron, who contended that the performance of an activity in private in one's own home obviates concerns of *uvdin de-chol* (see *Kuntres Ahavat Shalom,* a pamphlet by the Maharsham appended to the back of the *Minchat Shabbat,* the Sefer of my paternal grandfather. For proof of this concept, see *Betzah* 28b, *Ma-hu le-harot*).

(The lenient position pertaining to a timer must relate to situations in which lights are not turned on or off when one opens or closes the dishwasher.)

CARRYING A CHILD ON THE SABBATH

Question: What should one do on Shabbat when a child who is already in a thoroughfare simply refuses to walk, and there is no *eruv*?

Response: Not too long ago I was on the Lower East Side on Shabbat in order to deliver the opening monthly Friday evening lecture at the Bialystoker Synagogue. As I was walking home the next morning after services, I witnessed the following scene.

A young child was sitting on the sidewalk, crying. Standing next to him was his mother, who was pleading with him to get up and start walking home. The area has no official *eruv* sanctioned by the local rabbinate that would permit carrying on the Sabbath. Therefore the mother, who was obviously religious, simply would not pick up the child and carry him home. The child ignored his mother's pleas and continued to cry. The mother, looking somewhat embarrassed, stood next to the child, pleading with him to stop crying and begin to walk home with her. Was there another option available?

My feeling is that in such a circumstance the mother should at least have picked up the child and attempted to console him while standing in one place. There is absolutely no sin in picking up something, or somebody, in *reshut ha-rabbim*, a major public thoroughfare, as long as one does not carry a minimum of four *amot*. (Thus, picking something up while standing still and then putting it down is not a violation of the prohibition against carrying on the Sabbath.) Picking the child up and holding him might have comforted him and encouraged him to start walking. To stand nearby while letting the child cry appears not only harsh but also shows halachic ignorance. If the mother is unable to coax the child into starting to walk, she has the option of carrying the child a distance of less than four *amot* and stopping. This procedure of carrying the child (walking less than four *amot* and stopping) can be repeated until they arrive near their home. Hopefully, the child will then be able to walk into the house by himself, since carrying from a public domain, in this case the street, into a private domain – their home – is forbidden regardless of the distance involved.

This is a tedious halachic method for carrying a child home. There is also a simpler way. My grandfather, the *Minchat Shabbat,* pointed out that in Europe many parents carried their children in the street on the Sabbath even when there was no *eruv.* He noted the following in defense of their behavior (*limud zechut*).

The Peri Megadim rules that on Shabbat a *shevut di-shevut bi-mekom mitzvah* is permissible. This means that if an action is potentially forbidden on the Sabbath only because of the combination of two distinct rabbinic ordinances and the action is performed for the sake of a mitzvah, it is permissible. It is well known that carrying a child who is able to walk is prohibited only by a rabbinic decree, since *chai nosei et atzmo* – a living being, especially a human being, carries itself. It is not a Biblical transgression. In addition, the majority of halachic scholars maintain that our streets are not a "Biblical public thoroughfare" (*reshut ha-rabbim de-oraita*). Our streets are designated as a *karmelit*, which means that carrying therein is prohibited only by rabbinic law. Thus, carrying a child in our streets on the Sabbath is prohibited only if we combine both rabbinic bans. Therefore, rules the Peri Megadim, it is permissible if it is done for the sake of a mitzvah (See *Orach Chayyim, Mishbetzot Zahav* 325:1).

The *Minchat Shabbat* noted an interesting nuance: An action that alleviates the pain or anguish (*tza'ar*) of a young child is comparable to the performance of a mitzvah. He states that this is the halachic source that supports the practice of carrying children in areas without an *eruv.* Though he notes that many sages, including the Magen Avraham (*Orach Chayyim* 308:71 and *Shulchan Aruch ha-Rav* 308:81) disagree with the decision of the Peri Megadim, one should not object to the behavior of parents who rely on this ruling and carry their children on Shabbat in areas without an *eruv.* The conclusion of the *Minchat Shabbat* is that while this legal loophole should not be advocated *le-chat'hila,* it can serve as a basis not to criticize those who are lenient and carry children in public on the Sabbath in communities that have no *eruv* (*Minchat Shabbat* 82:28) or in an urgent situation, like that described above. In Europe, the Hassidic world accepted the Minchat Shabbat as a halachic authority for Shabbat observance.

Another important point: many years ago, Ha-Rav ha-Gaon R. Menachem Kasher ruled that one may carry on the Sabbath throughout the entire island of Manhattan. At that time the Aggudat Ha-Rabbonim and many Roshei Yeshiva disagreed with Rav Kasher. In recent years the Manhattan *eruv* was repaired, and it is examined every week before Shabbat. On the Upper East Side of Manhattan, for example, the congregants of all major Orthodox synagogues openly carry on the Sabbath and rely on the *eruv*, with the sanction of their rabbis. The *eruv* includes the Lower East Side of Manhattan. If the Minchat Shabbat ruled that one may not object to parents carrying children in areas without an *eruv* altogether, one certainly should not criticize those who carry children on the Lower East Side of Manhattan, which is included in the Manhattan *eruv*, even if local rabbis have not formally sanctioned carrying in the area.

My position is that if a child walks by himself and then refuses to walk any further and starts to cry, that is a *bedi-avad* (a situation after the fact) even for those who do not wish to sanction the *eruv*. Therefore, one may rely on the opinions of the *Peri Megadim* and the *Minchat Shabbat*, especially in Manhattan, and carry the child home.

Those who disagree have every right to do so, but they have no right to criticize.

PART IV

GENERAL SHABBAT CONCERNS

ATTENDANCE OF A MOURNER AT A SHABBAT BAR MITZVAH PARTY

Question: May a person observing the year of mourning for a deceased parent attend a bar mitzvah celebration on Shabbat?

Response: Yes. Even authorities that would forbid a mourner to attend a bar mitzvah party for a relative on a weekday would grant permission for attendance on Shabbat.

A mourner is definitely not at peace or manifesting complete harmony. Therefore, the *Shulchan Aruch* rules that greeting a mourner with the word *shalom* is prohibited (*Yoreh De'ah* 385:1). What constitutes prohibited behavior? The Gilyon Marasha (*Yoreh De'ah* 385:1) suggests that this law refers to the use of the word "shalom," which signifies the love of God. Before prayer one may not greet people with "shalom." This prohibition refers to the use of God's name (*Orach Chayyim* 89:2), although it is permissible to say "Good morning." Therefore, contends the Gilyon Maharshah, the same principle should apply to a mourner. Namely, the word "Shalom" is not to be used, but a greeting is to be allowed. The *Aruch HaShulchan* overtly rules that the word "shalom" should not be used at all in the home of the mourner (*Yoreh De'ah* 384:4).

Based upon the principle that greeting a mourner with the word "shalom" is prohibited, the Codes note that on Shabbat great authorities, including the Rambam, contend that such a greeting is permitted, since on Shabbat there is no public observance of mourning. Since the prohibition against using the word "shalom" falls within the category of public mourning, it is permitted on Shabbat. The Rama notes that those who contend that it is forbidden even on Shabbat would also forbid a mourner from receiving presents on Shabbat. According to those who permit a greeting with the word "shalom" on Shabbat, says the Rama, a mourner may receive gifts (*Yoreh De'ah* 385:4). The Taz cites the prohibition against gifts and adds the comment (see Bach) that a mourner also should not invite guests or attend [a party] at someone else's home on Shabbat (*Yoreh De'ah* 385:1).

It is evident that a halachic domino process permeates the noted prohibitions. Those who hold that one may not greet a mourner with the word "shalom" on Shabbat also contend that a mourner may not receive presents or visit with friends on Shabbat. However, should one hold with the general consensus that greeting a mourner with the word "shalom" is permitted on Shabbat, then accepting gifts and visiting the homes of friends is also permitted. According to this position, mourners may eat meals outside their own homes on Shabbat and invite friends to their homes on Shabbat.

Now, if it is permitted to extend "shalom" to a mourner on Shabbat – for otherwise it is deemed an act of public mourning, which is not allowed – then the refusal to attend the bar mitzvah of a relative should certainly be forbidden as public mourning. An uncle who does not attend the bar mitzvah of his nephew because of mourning is definitely a case of mourning *be-farhesia* (publicly), which, authorities note, does not follow accepted Halacha or practice.

GIVING BIRTH ON SHABBAT

Question: Does the psychological status of a mother giving birth have halachic ramifications?

Response: Yes. The Talmud notes several acts that may be performed on Shabbat for the sake of a mother about to give birth. It is written, "If she needs a lamp, her neighbor may kindle a lamp for her." The Talmud comments, "That is obvious." Rashi contends that the obvious law is that a mother about to give birth is classified as one with a life-threatening condition (*pikuach nefesh*), which supersedes Shabbat.

So why is it necessary to state explicitly that a friend may kindle a light for the woman in labor? The Talmud responds that the uniqueness of this law is that it deals with a woman who is blind. "You might argue, since she [the mother] cannot see it, it is forbidden. Therefore, he informs us that [we permit the kindling] to soothe her mind. [As] she reasons: If there is anything [required], my friend will see it and do it for me" (*Shabbat* 128b). In other words, one may kindle a light, which is actually a Biblical violation, to ease the distress of a blind woman about to give birth.

Tosafot hone this law further. For example, they note that on Yom Kippur a person may eat, providing a physician ordered that he must do so in order to save his life (*Yoma* 83a). Yet the Talmud appears to permit the violation of Shabbat merely to calm the mother. Tosafot conclude that the life of a woman about to give birth could be endangered if she should be frightened that those around her, friends or professionals, are not caring for her needs. Therefore, Biblical prohibitions that we normally observe on Shabbat may be violated in order to prevent her from having such fears.

Indeed, the Bach rules that at dusk, one may light candles for the woman in labor even if she has not asked for them. The Bi'ur Halacha notes other considerations, citing the Rambam, who relates the law to a time frame of occurrence. If a woman cries out in pain before her uterus has opened in preparation for birth, then lights are kindled only when she asks for them. However, once a woman's uterus is open, lights are kindled whether she

135

requests them or not because she is considered to be a patient whose life is potentially in danger.

The *Aruch ha-Shulchan* was concerned with the rule that work done on Shabbat for the sake of a laboring woman must be performed with a *shinui*, with altering the normal mode of action (*Orach Chayyim* 330:1). This prevents the violation of a Biblical law. In general, when danger to life is involved, the rule is that saving the life is of such importance that even great sages should be involved in violating the Sabbath in order to do so. Why, then, should we use a *shinui* in the case of a woman in labor? If a woman about to give birth is deemed to be in danger of her life, why should we care whether the violation of Shabbat that we perform on her behalf is of a Biblical or rabbinic nature?

The *Aruch ha-Shulchan* contends that giving birth is qualitatively different from other forms of imminent danger to life. It is natural to give birth. Most women bear the birthing process with its accompanying pain, because they realize that it will pass and that the child will be born and the pain will cease. Therefore, under normal circumstances, the act of giving birth, in and of itself, does not endanger a woman's life. For this reason, under normal circumstances, a *shinui* is the preferred mode. However, it may still be life-threatening. If we see that the mother is anxious and more fearful than other women, then we may kindle a light for her even if she is blind because the fear itself could harm her (*Aruch ha-Shulchan, Orach Chayyim* 330:2). Accordingly, a birthing mother's emotional agitation definitely would impact the halachic reaction to her condition.

Please note that the above discussion relates to a woman in labor, before the actual process of birth itself. When a woman is actually giving birth, her case is clearly considered one of *pikuach nefesh*.

MAKING MUSICAL SOUNDS ON SHABBAT

Question: Years ago, as rav of the Mizrachi Kehilla in Melbourne, Australia, I was usually granted the honor of reciting *ha-motzi* over *lechem mishneh* aloud at the third Shabbat meal at the synagogue (seudat shlishit). Since there was usually a large crowd and it was quite noisy, I frequently took the *challa* knife and tapped on a glass or bottle in order to silence everyone before I recited the berachah. Was this action permissible on Shabbat?

Response: A unique aspect of serving as the *mara de-atra* of a large Orthodox congregation composed mainly of observant Jews was that almost every nuance of my behavior was constantly scrutinized and subject to halachic analysis. I knew that sooner or later, someone would ask for the halachic rationale behind my customs and behavior. Therefore, I realized that all my actions had to be supported by halachic sources. So: was my tapping on the glass permissible?

The general halacha is that on Shabbat, one may not use or play any item or instrument specifically set up for musical purposes (see Shulchan Aruch, *Orach Chayyim, Hilchot Shabbat* 338:1 – *Kitzur Shulchan Aruch* 80:88). The concern is that *hashma'at kol* – generating (or increasing) certain sounds – is prohibited only when the sounds emanate from an instrument or item specifically designed to produce or increase sound. Commenting upon this limiting factor, my paternal grandfather, the Minchat Shabbat, ruled that the custom of tapping a knife together with, for example, a fork in order to signal servants in a second room that it is time to serve the next course of the meal is halachically permissible. Why?

The process does not entail usage of a *keli meyuchad le-shir* – namely, it did not deal with either instruments or items specifically set up for music (*Minchat Shabbat* 80:246) Therefore, tapping on a glass with a knife should also be permissible and not be a cause for halachic concern.

TAKING PILLS ON SHABBAT

Question: To alleviate a medical condition, a doctor prescribed pills for a patient. The patient started ingesting the daily pills prior to Shabbat. He was told that if he should skip a day, the medicine will be ineffective. May he take the pill on Shabbat?

Response: The Talmud relates a case in which a person had taken a medicine on Thursday and Friday. On Shabbat he needed to dissolve and drink it. The Talmud rules that since he had drunk it on Thursday and Friday, he is permitted to dissolve and drink it on Shabbat, since otherwise his life would be in danger (*Shabbat* 140a). The obvious implication is that this activity is permissible only in a life threatening condition.

Ha-Gaon ha-Rav R. Yosef Shalom Elyashiv noted the following distinction. The Talmudic example deals with a case where some preparation is necessary to make the medicine effective. Indeed, there is a position that to dissolve medicine even in cold water violates a rabbinical prohibition. In this situation, the rabbis allowed it only when not taking the medicine would endanger life.

Taking pills on Shabbat is a completely different matter. The patient does not need to do anything to the pills themselves. The only concern is the general decree forbidding the use of medicine because of the fear that one may grind the ingredients and prepare medicine (*shechikat samemanim*). Since the patient is not performing any forbidden action upon the medicine itself and had already begun the medical process on Friday, he may be allowed to continue on Shabbat. In other words, perhaps the rabbis never imposed a prohibition in such a situation (see *Kovetz Teshuvot* 40, ruling cited in the name of Ha-Rav Shlomo Kluger, *Sefer ha-Chayyim* 328:10).

LEARNING THE LAWS OF SHABBAT
ON THE SHABBAT

Question: Is it a *mitzvah* to learn the laws of Shabbat on the Sabbath?

Response: The Talmud cites the verse, "Moshe announced God's festivals to the Children of Israel" (Vayikra 23:44). The Talmud (*Megillah* 32a) says that this indicates that it is an obligation to read the Torah portion pertaining to each festival at its proper time. *Tanu rabbanan* – the sages taught that Moshe decreed that they should inquire and expound about the matters of the day, referring to the laws of Pesach on Pesach, the laws of Shavuot on Shavuot, and the laws of Sukkot on Sukkot.

Rashi explains the Talmudic citation as follows. The verse appears to be extraneous, since Moshe taught the Israelites all the mitzvot, not only the laws pertaining to the holidays. Therefore, why does the Torah emphasize the fact the Moshe taught the festivals to the Israelites? Rashi says that the verse teaches us that Moshe would teach the people the laws of each festival on the festival itself.

The Biblical section that tells the Israelites how to observe the various festivals includes a section pertaining to the laws of Shabbat (*Yayikra* 23:3). The *Sefat Emet* overtly notes that Moshe's command to teach the laws of each particular festival on that festival also applies to Shabbat. Just as one is required to study the laws of Pesach on Pesach, one must study the laws of Shabbat on Shabbat. His argument is that the verse that begins *Va-yedaber Moshe* refers to all the previous verses about the holidays as well as with Shabbat, which is included within that section.

Moreover, The Sefat Emat wonders about R. Yehoshua b. Levi's ruling that if Purim should fall on Shabbat, one must discuss the laws of Purim on that day (*Megillah* 4a). Indeed, if there is an obligation to discuss the laws of Shabbat on Shabbat, why should the laws of Purim take precedence over those of Shabbat? He suggests that perhaps Purim takes precedence because it is a mitzvah that applies only for a short period, while there are many opportunities throughout the year to observe and learn about Shabbat. He also provides other distinctions, such as that Purim includes the special mitzvah of *pirsum ha-nes*, publicizing the miracle. He does not however retract his position that there is a special mitzvah on Shabbat to learn or teach the laws of Shabbat itself.

This suggests that *shiurim* (classes) should be held on Shabbat to learn about Shabbat itself.

TWO-DAY HOLIDAYS: SHABBAT AND SUNDAY

Question: Whenever a Yom Tov falls on Shabbat and/or Sunday, synagogues generally forego the *seudah,* or light meal, that they usually hold after *Mincha* on Shabbat afternoon. What is the rationale for eliminating the *seudah* held in the synagogue? Since Halacha requires us to eat three meals on Shabbat, there seems to be no reason to eliminate this mitzvah on a Shabbat afternoon on the first day of a Yom Tov that comes out on Shabbat or Sunday.

Reponse: Eliminating *seudah shelishit* (the third meal) in the synagogue does not mean that one should not eat this meal on the first day of Yom Tov that comes out on Shabbat. Indeed, Halacha maintains that one should eat a third meal on the first day of a Yom Tov that falls out on Shabbat. It is suggested that in such a case, one may fulfill this mitzvah by washing once again right after lunch, making the blessing over bread, and then reciting *birkat ha-mazon.* By using this option, everyone may observe the mitzvah of the third meal on Shabbat.

What does not occur on the Shabbat of the first day of a Yom Tov is the public synagogue meal generally observed between *Mincha* and *Maariv.* This is based on the following halachic rule. The Shulchan Aruch states that it is forbidden to eat a *seudah* on Friday afternoon as a mark of respect for Shabbat. The basic reason for this prohibition is that not having a meal enables one to have an appetite to enjoy the meal on Friday night (*Orach Chayyim* 249:2). The Mishna Berurah cites the Peri Megadim, who states that this prohibition is applicable even on the eve of Yom Tov, since there is a mitzvah of *oneg Yom Tov* – to make the day enjoyable and to honor it (*Mishna Berurah, Orach Chayyim* 349:8).

Just as one should not eat a meal right before Shabbat, one should also refrain from doing so on erev Yom Tov. This ensures that one have an appetite and look forward to the Yom Tov meal. Accordingly, based upon the above rule, synagogues do not serve *seudah shelishit* after *Mincha* on Shabbat on the first day of Yom Tov. However, congregants should be advised to eat the third meal earlier in the day.

BIRKAT KOHANIM ON SHABBAT OF A YOM TOV

Question: When Yom Tov occurs on Shabbat, some Diaspora communities hold *birkat Kohanim* while others do not. Why should Shabbat in any way alter the normal obligation for the Kohanim to bless the people?

Response: The rationale for not observing Birkat Kohanim when Yom Tov occurs on Shabbat is as follows: In ancient times, the Kohanim would immerse in a mikevh before the blessing. It is also well known that on Friday night it is a traditional mitzvah for married couples to be intimate with each other. Accordingly, on Shabbat morning the Kohanim would generally not have had an opportunity to immerse in a mikveh after having sexual relations the previous evening. Since the sages did not want the Kohanim to recite the blessing without going to the mikveh first, they simply eliminated the blessing altogether when Yom Tov fell on Shabbat (See *Magen Avraham, Orach Chayyim* 128:70).

Although the *Kitzur Shulchan Aruch* cites both customs, it rules that it is preferable for Kohanim to recite the blessing when Yom Tov falls on Shabbat (*Kitzur Shulchan Aruch,* Hilchot Yom Tov 100:1. See also Taz, *se'if katan* 38 and *Shulchan Aruch Ha-Rav,* paragraph 57, who concur). Indeed, simple, pragmatic logic suggests that no synagogue in modern times requires Kohanim to immerse in a mikveh before duchening. No one ever questions Kohanim concerning such personal matters. Many synagogues that did not hold Birkat Kohanim on Shabbat reviewed the issue and reinstated it. The prevalent custom on Shabbat is that the Kohanim do not sing extra niggunim, and the congregation responds "amen" immediately after each verse of Birkat Kohanim.

CARRYING BY MISTAKE ON SHABBAT

Question: A person leaves his home and while walking in the street becomes aware he is carrying something in his pocket. What should he do?

Response: The assumption is that the area is not enclosed by an *eruv*. This incident may involve two violations of Shabbat: transferring an item from a private to a public domain, and carrying an item more than four *amot* in a public domain. Accordingly, a method must be devised to avoid or lessen each potential violation.

The first mishna of Tractate Shabbat mentions the prohibition of carrying items from a private domain to a public thoroughfare. It notes that the process of transferring items (*hotza'ah* or *hachnasah*) entails two distinct actions: *akira* – picking the item up from a stationary position, and *hanacha* – placing the item in a stationary position. If both actions should be performed, this is considered a violation of Biblical law. Should one of these actions be performed it would be prohibited only rabbinically. If neither action occurs, then no violation transpires. In addition, in order to violate Shabbat, one must be aware of what one is doing at the time the activity begins.

The Talmud says: "If one is laden with food and drink and goes in and out all day (from private to public ground), he is liable only when he stands still. Said Abaye: Providing that he stands still to rest" (*Shabbat* 5b). Rashi provides the following rationale. The person laden with food had no intention to transfer items from a private to a public domain. He simply wanted to carry items from one area in a home to another. Later on, he decided to go out. But he never had stopped to stand still. He was constantly moving. In order to violate Shabbat, one must emulate the service at the Mishkan (the Tabernacle in the wilderness), which was a deliberate, conscious process. Indeed, whenever one does not intend to violate Shabbat, one is not liable. Therefore, if one did not pick up the item in order to carry it outside the house, this would also not be a violation of Shabbat. Moreover, as long as the person never stopped moving, the action lacked both *akira* and *hanacha* (see also Tosafot 3b).

Based upon the above, one may resolve the dilemma of a person who realized that he, or she, was carrying on Shabbat by accident. First, the one carrying the item had not picked it up with intent to do so, and did not realize that he was carrying anything. Indeed, when the person left his home he was unaware that he was carrying anything. Therefore, there is no *akira*. The moment the person stands still or stops, this constitutes *hanacha* without *akira* which, while it is not a scriptural violation, it is a rabbinic one. *Akira* without *hanacha,* or vice versa, may not be performed on Shabbat (*Shabbat* 3a).

Yet the Talmud (5b) specifically notes that when *akira* does not take place, one may return home. Why? As long as the person did not stop, there would be no *hanacha.* If he were to return home without stopping, no violation would take place because carrying with no *akira* or *hanacha* is permitted rabbinically. So the most viable suggestion to a person who accidentally became aware that he was carrying an object is to go back home, or to his original place of departure, without stopping, and unload the object there.

CARRYING A TALIT

Question: A person lives in an area enclosed by an *eruv*. If he carried his tallit to the synagogue in order to wear it during services, may he carry it home afterwards? If he will have no further need for the tallit on Shabbat, should he be permitted to carry it home after davening?

Response: The *Shulchan Aruch* rules that in order to move an item on Shabbat or Yom Tov, there must be a reason to do so. Without such a need, one may not move the item. However, it may be handled and moved to prevent its being lost or stolen (*Shulchan Aruch Orach Chayyim* 308:4).

From the above halacha, it is clear that if a person is apprehensive that unless he takes his tallit home on Shabbat it may be lost or stolen, then he may carry it home with him.

The *Aruch ha-Shulchan* provides the rationale for this leniency. Something that one may use on Shabbat is not *muktzeh*. However, some rabbinic scholars are stringent even regarding these items and require a specific purpose for them on Shabbat. Yet since the items are not essentially *muktzeh*, any form of *ta'anug* (personal pleasure or emotional need) suffices to permit their use (*Aruch ha-Shulchan* 308:15). My grandfather, the Minchat Shabbat, agrees, citing the Shelah ha-Kodesh, who notes that every item that is moved or carried on Shabbat should have a *tzorech mah* – some sort of purpose – for Shabbat itself. The Minchat Shabbat interprets the latter phrase to mean any form of a need, even if it is minor. Indeed, this is the general rule. Moreover, the Minchat Shabbat notes that in his era many have the custom to move and carry items even without any need at all. He contends that this leniency is based on those sages who hold that once an item may be moved on Shabbat, it may be moved and carried without any purpose at all. Though this is common practice, it is not the preferable *minhag*. One should be careful that there is some purpose in moving the item (*Minchat Shabbat* 88:53).

CARRYING KEYS ON SHABBAT

Question: On Shabbat, in an area enclosed by an *eruv,* or on Yom Tov, may one carry a key ring that contains both house and car keys?

Response: Ha-Rav ha-Gaon Rav Moshe Feinstein *ʒ"l* ruled that on Yom Tov, a person who generally smokes ten cigarettes during a period of time that he is away from his home could carry a full pack containing twenty cigarettes (*Iggrot Moshe, Orach Chayyim* II:103). Based upon this ruling, the Shemirat Shabbat ke-Hilchata stated that one may also carry a key ring that includes keys that are not used on Shabbat. The rationale is that the key ring is comparable to the pack of cigarettes. Just as Rav Moshe Feinstein ruled that one may carry the entire pack of cigarettes without removing in advance the number of cigarettes that the person will not smoke, one may carry a key ring that contains certain keys that are not used on Shabbat or Yom Tov (*Shemirat Shabbat ke-Hilchata,* Chapter 19, 6:17).

When Rav Feinstein reviewed this issue later, he ruled that one may not carry (in an area with an *eruv* or on Yom Tov) a key ring containing keys that will not be used during such periods of time. Moreover, he noted that the case of the car key is distinctly different from that of the cigarettes. In the latter situation, each individual cigarette may be smoked. Therefore, one may carry the entire packet. The case of the key ring deals with keys, such as car keys, that will not be used at all. They should therefore be removed prior to Shabbat or Yom Tov (*Iggrot Moshe* Vol. 8, *Orach Chayyim,* V:35). The implication is that the car keys acquire the status of *muktzeh.*

Note: This decision of Ha-Rav Moshe was in a period of time that many were unaware of the extent of danger to health of smoking. Current rabbinic position is that one should not smoke at all.

TIMING OF A *SHALOM ZACHAR* AND *SIMCHAT BAT*

Question: A boy was born on Friday night after Shabbat began. There is no halachic doubt that the *brit milah* will be held on the morning of the following Shabbat. When should the *shalom zachar* be held? Should it be planned for the first Friday night after the birth or for the subsequent Friday night, before the *brit milah*?

Response: The *Peri Megadim* cites the *Terumat ha-Deshen*, who rules that the *shalom zachar* should be observed on the first Friday night and may not be delayed a week to the Friday night directly before the circumcision. The rationale is that one of the motivations for the celebration of a *shalom zachar* is the joy that parents feel over the fact that the child was born. It is the celebration of the miracle of birth. The child is alive. Accordingly, the *shalom zachar* should take place as close as possible to the actual birth rather than the *brit milah* (*Peri Megadim, Orach Chayyim* 444; *Mishbetzot Zahav* 9).

The following tends to corroborate this ruling. An ancient midrash notes that the Fifth Commandment is dependent upon the Fourth Commandment. The Fifth Commandment is the mitzvah of honoring parents. The Fourth Commandment is the mitzvah to observe the Sabbath. The connection is that if God had not ceased His creation on Shabbat, then human beings would not have had the ability to have children. Each successive generation would be a creative act of God. The very fact that God stopped His work of creation on Shabbat means that humans were now granted the power of creation. Therefore, the mitzvah of honoring parents is a result of the mitzvah of Shabbat.

This may be a basic reason why a *shalom zachar* is celebrated on Shabbat: the recognition that the *mitzvah* of *Shabbat* is the source for the power to give birth. Thus, it would appear more proper to have the celebration on the Shabbat closest to the birth and not necessarily right before the *brit milah*.

The same reasons should apply to the celebration upon the birth of a girl. The purpose of such a celebration, known in some circles as a *simchat bat,* is to link the miracle of birth to the mitzvah of Shabbat and to express gratitude to God. This suggests that the event should be held as closely as possible to the birth. Though the *simchat bat* is a more recent ceremony, it certainly cannot be wrong to call people together to thank God for the miracle of birth. On the contrary, it is a form of *kiddush ha-shem*.

THE *AUFRUF*

Question: What is the purpose of the *aufruf*? Why is it the (Ashkenazi) custom to call a bridegroom to the Torah before his wedding?

Response: A unique reason may be derived from a Biblical verse.

In Bamidbar, the Torah states: "They assembled the whole congregation on the first day of the second month, and they declared themselves according to their birth, after their families after the house of their forefathers, according to the number of the names from twenty years upwards, by their polls" (Bamidbar 1:18 translation, Samson Raphael Hirsch). Rashi notes that everyone brought records to substantiate their lineage. This process had to take place in front of the entire assembly of the Israelites. Why was it important for everyone to be present when individuals attested to their lineage from specific families and tribes?

Rav Yehonatan Eibshitz suggests that the public nature of the process was essential to the verification of all claims. Since everyone was present when lineage was proclaimed, members of the assembly who wished to question a particular claim would be able to do so. If there was silence when a claim was made, it was taken as consent (*Commentary on the Torah*). This tradition of using a public assembly in order to substantiate a given family lineage goes back to ancient times.

The *aufruf* may be a comparable vehicle. It is a form of a public announcement stating that a specific Jewish man is about to marry a specific Jewish woman. The public nature of the event allows for anyone who could possibly question the halachic legality of the marriage to do so before the wedding. If no one does, this is taken to mean that no one questions the impending union. Silence implies consent.

It is told that certain Hassidic rebbes maintained that there is a reason why a *chatan* is called up to the Torah before and after his wedding. The purpose of the *aliyah* before the wedding is to convey the message to the groom that his married life should be based upon Torah values. The *aliyah* after marriage is intended to instruct the groom that the Torah does not change now that he is married. It is the same Torah that it always was.

A WRISTWATCH ON SHABBAT

Question: May one wear a wristwatch on Shabbat in an area that does not contain an *eruv*?

Response: In the halachic rulings of the Shemirat Shabbat ke-Hilchata (Chapter 18: *se'if* 26, and *se'if katan* 45) Ha-Rav Shlomo Zalman Auerbach is quoted as saying that since the wristwatch is worn regularly, it is considered as part of one's clothing. Therefore, it may be worn on Shabbat even in areas that have no *eruv*.

Rav Auerbach was asked to clarify his ruling further: did Halacha permit one to wear a wristwatch in an area without an *eruv*, or did the Rav mean to suggest that one should not protest against those who wore them on Shabbat? Rav Auerbach responded that he believed that it was permissible according to the halacha (*Al pi din, le-chat'hilah*). Yet there was also support if one wished to be stringent (*Ve-aleihu lo yibbol: Customs of HaRav Shlomo Zalman Auerbach,* I:220).

SHACHARIT OR MUSAF?

Question: A person commemorating a *yahrzeit* is given the choice of serving as *sheliach tzibbur* for either *Shacharit* or *Musaf.* Which one should he choose?

Response: This question was posed to Ha-Rav Shmuel Dovid ha-Kohen Munk of Haifa, Israel. Rav Munk's ruling was that preference should be given to leading services for *Shacharit.* The rationale presented was that *Shacharit* entailed reciting more prayers that elicit responses from the congregation than *Musaf* does. For example, "There are the responses of 'amen' to the blessings of Keriat Shema; the response of Barchu and the fact that in *Shacharit* the *sheliach tzibbur* recites Kaddish more times than at *Musaf*" (Responsa *Pe'at ha-Sadeh,* Part II, Orach Chayyim 94:2).

Rav Munk's statement that the sheliach tzibbur for *Shacharit* recites the Kaddish more often than at *Musaf* seems inaccurate at first. An examination of *Shacharit* shows that the *sheliach tzibbur* by himself, not counting the mourners' Kaddish, recites Kaddish only twice; once before Barchu and once after the Amidah. In *Musaf* the *sheliach tzibbur* also recites Kaddish twice: once prior to the Amida, and once after the Amida. As such, in both occasions, the *sheliach tzibbur* recites by himself Kaddish the same amount. Moreover, if we include the Kaddish recited by mourners, then *Musaf* provides the *sheliach tzibbur* with many more opportunities than *Shacharit* does. Presuming that the *sheliach tzibbur* begins at *Shacharit* and not with the preliminary morning blessings, the *sheliach tzibbur* does not recite the Mourners' Kaddish even once. At *Musaf,* the Mourners' Kaddish is recited after Aleinu, the Psalm of the Day, and some after Anim Zemirot (according to *minhag Ashkenaz*).

A possible response is that mention may be made of the additional Kaddish recited on Shabbat, before *maftir,* and on Mondays and Thursdays at the Torah reading. Although in general the reader recites this Kaddish, there is a custom to grant a mourner the right to say it. Since the *baal shacharit* who is commemorating a *yahrzeit* may be also granted maftir and is standing near the Sefer Torah, most probably he would be given the honor to recite this

Kaddish. Then there would be more opportunities for a *sheliach tzibbur* for *Shacharit* to recite Kaddish than at *Musaf.*

ALEINU LESHABE'ACH

Question: The prevalent custom is to recite the *Aleinu* on Shabbat after the *Musaf* service. Why do we not recite *Aleinu* at the end of *Shacharit*?

Response: In general, *Aleinu* is recited throughout the week at the end of each daily prayer service. We would expect that the practice would be the same on Shabbat. Why is *Aleinu* not recited after *Shacharit* on Shabbat or on Yom Tov?

The Tur *(Shulchan Aruch, Orach Chayyim* 133) notes that *Aleinu* is recited at the end of the morning services. However, he mentions no requirement to recite it after *Mincha* or *Maariv*. Rama also notes *(Orach Chayyim* 133:2) that *Aleinu* is recited upon the conclusion of the morning prayers, also with no mention of any obligation to do so after *Mincha* or *Maariv*. The *Mishna Berurah (Orach Chayyim* 132:7) cites the Ari as the (Kabbalistic) source for the common custom to recite *Aleinu* also after *Mincha* and *Maariv*. If the *Maariv* service takes place early, directly after *Mincha,* as is generally done in large congregations, the *Mishna Berurah* rules that *Aleinu* is not recited after *Mincha*. In this case, it is sufficient to recite it after *Maariv*. Indeed, this latter custom was the practice in German synagogues.

Accordingly, the recitation of *Aleinu* developed in stages. First it was only recited after *Shacharit,* and only later was it added after *Mincha* and *Maariv*. The Bach presents a plausible rationale for the original obligation to recite *Aleinu:* as Jews left the synagogue to go about their business in the Gentile world, it strengthened their faith and protected the purity of their belief (Tur, *loc. cit.*). This is the reason that it was originally intended for the end of the morning services. After *Mincha* and *Maariv,* Jews usually went home and had no further contact with the outside world. Therefore, the Sages felt no need to impose any special safeguards for Jewish values at that time. This is why they did not require the recitation of *Aleinu* between *Shacharit* and *Musaf:* as long as Jews remained in the synagogue, there was no need for extra prayers to protect them from the influences of the outside world.

This may also be the rationale for the German synagogue custom not to say *Aleinu* after *Mincha* when it was immediately followed by *Maariv*. Though the Ari felt that *Aleinu* should be recited after each daily prayer service for Kabbalistic reasons. Rabbis in general may have felt that whenever each of the three major daily prayers concludes and Jews enter the sphere of normal, worldly life, they need additional prayers to bolster their spiritual state.

A TRICYCLE ON SHABBAT

Question: May a minor ride a tricycle on Shabbat within an *eruv*?

Response: The Debritziner Rav, Rav Moshe Stern, ruled that a minor may ride a tricycle, but not a bicycle, on Shabbat. He contended that children below the age of *chinuch* may ride tricycles, and no one should protest. Above the age of *chinuch*, it is preferable not to ride a tricycle, but (*al pi din*) parents need not restrain children from doing so. (The tricycle bell should be removed or disabled on Shabbat.) However, adults may not ride bicycles on Shabbat or Yom Tov for the following reasons: they may break down and one may violate Shabbat by fixing them, and they are *uvda de-chol*, not in the spirit of Shabbat (see Responsa, Be'er Moshe, Vol. VI, Responsum 16).

DANCING ON SHABBAT AT SHEVA BERACHOT

Question: Is dancing permitted during the celebration of an *aufruf* or at a *sheva berachot* that is held on Shabbat?

Response: The *Shulchan Aruch* rules that dancing is prohibited on Shabbat. However, the Rama notes that many people dance on Shabbat and no one protests. He presents two reasons for this: since people will not heed any prohibitions against dancing it is better for them to transgress unwittingly than deliberately, and the underlying reason it is not allowed is because one may become so emotionally aroused that he may build a musical instrument. Since most are unable to build musical instruments, in reality it appears that the prohibition does not apply (*Orach Chayyim* 339:3).

There was a time when all forms of dancing were forbidden on Shabbat. This prohibition was altered later on because of the two reasons presented by the Rama. Yet even when the custom was to outlaw dancing on Shabbat, dancing was still allowed on Simchat Torah. The *Mishna Berurah* contends that dancing on Simchat Torah was permitted for the sake of *kevod ha-Torah.* Yet dancing is forbidden at the simcha of other mitzvot that are not connected to *kevod ha-Torah,* such as a wedding (*Mishna Berurah,* 339:8). The latter phrase of the *Mishna Berurah* is difficult to understand, since marriages are not even permitted on Shabbat. Perhaps the *Mishna Berurah* is alluding to an *aufruf* or *sheva berachot* that takes place on Shabbat. Thus, dancing is permitted only for *kevod ha-Torah,* and not for other mitzvot.

In noting the Rama's final ruling, which is lenient about dancing on Shabbat, the Mishna Berurah adds the comment that it is not proper to permit dancing on Shabbat unless one is observing a mitzvah in the process. When no mitzvah is being fulfilled, dancing is permitted only because it is better to sin unintentionally than deliberately (*Mishna Berurah* 339:10).

Here the Mishna Berurah alters his language. Dancing needs not only a situation of *kevod ha-Torah,* but it is also permitted while performing an ordinary mitzvah. Indeed, there is no limitation or definition of the type of mitzvah whose fulfillment would allow for dancing. Therefore, the following procedure develops. At one time in history, dancing was forbidden on Shabbat except in order to honor the Torah (for example, on Simchat Torah). Later on, dancing was allowed on Shabbat, though no blanket permission was granted. It was necessary to perform a mitzvah in the process (such as *sheva berachot* or gladdening a newly-married couple). If no mitzvah was being fulfilled at that particular time, dancing would still be allowed, but only on the grounds that it is better to sin unintentionally than deliberately. A *ben Torah* would certainly not use such a leniency.

In a discussion of the laws of Rosh Chodesh, the Mishna Berurah, in his compendium of sources entitled *Shaar ha-Tzion,* discusses why Kiddush Levana (the prayer sanctifying the new moon) is not recited on Friday night. He suggests that as many people recite Kiddush Levana, they dance, which is not allowed on Shabbat. The fact that dancing is allowed on Simchat Torah is not considered a challenge to his position. The reason for this is that while Kiddush Levana may be set up before or after Shabbat, Simchat Torah has a set date (*Shaar ha-Tzion, Orach Chayyim* 426:11).

Of concern is the apparent question posed by dancing on Simchat Torah. Although the Mishna Berurah could have answered that dancing is permitted only for *kevod ha-Torah,* but not for other mitzvot, it does not do so. Since an *aufruf* or a *sheva berachot* are events that take place on Shabbat and cannot be moved to another day, the logical inference is that dancing is permitted on Shabbat to gladden the bride and groom.

Reliable sources report that Ha-Gaon Rav Shneur Kotler, *z"l,* danced on Shavuot. He maintained that this was the custom of his father, Ha-Gaon Rav Aaron Kotler, *z"l.*

There is also a Limmud Zechut to the many minyanim that dance during Shabbat prayers (for example the Carlebach-style ones). Once dancing was permitted to enhance a Mitzvah, then all forms of dancing that generage greater enthusiasm for Tefilla became permitted.

SHABBAT TESHUVAH

Question: The Sabbath between Rosh Hashanah and Yom Kippur is called Shabbat Teshuvah because it is when the *haftarah,* which begins with Hosea 14:2 – *"Shuvah, Yisrael"* ("Return, O Israel" or, in another meaning, "Repent, O Israel") – is recited (see *Matteh Moshe* 893). Might this suggest that this particular Sabbath has nothing to do with *teshuvah* in and of itself, but received its name because of its *haftarah* or because it falls so soon before Yom Kippur?

Response: No. It may be demonstrated that the observance of Shabbat has a great deal to do with repentance. The Talmud (*Shabbat* 118b) cites the words of R. Yochanan: "Whosoever observes the Sabbath according to all its laws is forgiven even if he practices idolatry like [the generation of] Enosh." This Talmudic statement puzzled the famed halachic commentator the Taz. Somehow it does not fit in with our understanding of the process of *teshuvah.*

The Talmud states that observing the Sabbath leads to repentance. Why? Did the person who observed the Sabbath do *teshuvah*? If he did, his sins should have been forgiven in any case. If he did not, then it is hard to understand why he should be granted forgiveness. How can forgiveness take place without *teshuvah*?

The response of the Taz crystallizes a unique role of Shabbat and its relationship to repentance. It is well known that *teshuvah* by itself does not always result in atonement. Some sins are considered to be so serious that *teshuvah* cannot atone for them. Indeed, the Talmud (*Yoma* 86a) rules that if one has committed a sin for which the punishment is *karet* or death at the hands of the *beit din* and he repented, then his repentance and Yom Kippur suspend the punishment, and suffering completes the atonement. The person who has sinned must suffer before being forgiven. The Taz suggests that perhaps R. Yochanan's statement (*Shabbat loc. cit.*) teaches us that the spiritual impact of Sabbath observance is so powerful that a sinner who repents need not suffer before he achieves atonement. The Sabbath, together with *teshuvah*, has the ability to grant atonement (Taz, *Orach Chayyim* 242:1).

The Taz's theory demonstrates that Sabbath observance may enhance *teshuvah*. In fact, Sabbath observance furnishes a means of atonement that not even Yom Kippur can provide. The Talmud (*Yoma, loc. cit.*) specifically rules that Yom Kippur and repentance cannot provide atonement for certain sins without personal suffering. Yet it appears that the Sabbath is somehow able, together with *teshuvah*, to atone for the same types of sins for which Yom Kippur, combined with *teshuvah,* do not.

This suggests that Shabbat Teshuvah is more than just a period of time to address the congregation about the approaching Yom Kippur. Shabbat Teshuvah is the last Sabbath before Yom Kippur that enables us to win atonement without the Divine punishment of anguish and suffering. Shabbat Teshuvah thus is an opportunity to do *teshuvah*. Jews must be informed that an unusual choice is available to all who wish to do *teshuvah*. If they repent on the Sabbath itself by not only doing *teshuvah* but by making certain to observe all the laws of the Sabbath properly and scrupulously, they may win atonement without personal suffering. If Jews wish to wait until Yom Kippur to do *teshuvah*, they may win atonement, but may still have to undergo personal suffering.

I am positive that awareness of this choice will result in Shabbat Teshuva becoming a day on which people do *teshuva,* not just a day of preparation for the Day of Atonement. The *haftara* is a call to Jews to use Shabbat itself for *teshuva.*

SHABBAT HA-GADOL

Question: Why is the Shabbat before Pesach commemorated as Shabbat ha-Gadol? Do the historical reasons for the celebration have anything to do with Shabbat itself?

Response: Tradition has it that the Sabbath before Passover is labeled Shabbat ha-Gadol, the Great Sabbath. This probably means that it is somehow more special than the others. Yet the rationale presented for commemorating this day as the Great Sabbath has nothing to do with the concept, symbol, or message of Shabbat.

Why do Jews celebrate this day? The Tur *Shulchan Aruch (Orach Chayyim* 430) reports that a great miracle took place at the time. On the tenth day of the Hebrew month of Nisan, which occurred on Shabbat, the Jews brought lambs to their homes in order to observe God's command to slaughter and eat them on the night of their deliverance from Egyptian bondage. Since the Egyptians worshiped lambs as deities, the penalty for slaughtering one was death. The miracle was that although Jews prepared these lambs for slaughter, the Egyptians did not harm them.

The joy of Jewish salvation was so great that we commemorate it on the Shabbat before Passover. The term "Shabbat ha-Gadol" refers to the miracle that took place in Egypt on the Shabbat before the Jews won their freedom.

The problem posed here is that Shabbat was incidental to the miracle. In order to remember the event, the sages should have established the tenth day of Nisan, not Shabbat, as a semi-holiday. Indeed, since the miracle occurred on Shabbat, then the exodus took place on the fifteenth day of Nisan, which fell on a Thursday. Yet no one pinpoints Thursday as a day of celebration. The motive for commemorating Shabbat ha-Gadol therefore appears questionable.

Ha-Rav Shlomo Kluger, in his commentary on the *Haggadah,* presents a unique theory that resolves these concerns. He contends that in Egypt, Shabbat, the seventh day, was generally considered a day of bad luck. Some people even fasted on Shabbat in order to counter its negative influence. The fact that the plagues started on Shabbat showed the Egyptians further proof that the seventh day was marked for evil and should be shunned as much as possible.

On the tenth day of Nisan, Jews obeyed God's commands and suffered no harm as a result. As the Jews tethered the lambs to posts and stated openly that they were to be slaughtered, they certainly must have feared retaliation. The fact that the incident took place on Shabbat, the day that the Egyptians abhorred, only increased the tension.

When no one attacked the Jews, it became apparent that Shabbat was a day of good fortune, at least for Jews. It was the first time in many years that Shabbat was celebrated as a day of joy. Therefore, the dawn of deliverance occurred on Shabbat, not the tenth day of Nisan. This day, which marked the beginning of the exodus, taught Jews that Shabbat is a day of pleasure, joy, and good fortune.

The *Aruch ha-Shulchan* reports that in ancient times, many Gentiles would insist upon keeping their homes dark on Shabbat in order to symbolize the evil forces of the day, according to contemporary astrological belief. The reason that Jews light their homes on Shabbat is in order to demonstrate that our fate is not ordained by the stars but by God (see *Orach Chayyim* 271:11).

Halacha chose to commemorate these events on Shabbat ha-Gadol in order to record the historical role that Shabbat played in the Jewish people's deliverance.

SAVING A JEW ON SHABBAT (I)

Question: Shabbat must be violated in order to save a person's life. Who should commit the violation in this case: adults, minors or Gentiles?

Response: The *Shulchan Aruch* rules that when Shabbat is violated in order to save a person's life, it is better that the action be performed by adults (*Yisrael gedolim*) rather than by children. However, the Rama modifies this rule, suggesting that where there is no loss of time it is preferable to have the action performed by a non-Jew or using a *shinui*. However, if one believes that the Gentile may not be careful or may delay, then it should be done only by a Jew (*Orach Chayyim* 328:12).

The *Mishna Berurah* notes that the Rama's rule is based on the principle that one does not violate Shabbat even for a *sakanah* (a life-threatening condition) when the act may be performed in a permitted manner (*se'if katan* 35). In addition, in situations where one may ask a Gentile to perform the act, one may also ask a minor (*se'if katan* 36). He cites the Taz, who disagrees with the Rama's position. The Taz contends that a Jew must perform the act in question because a Jew will be more zealous in doing so.

The *Mishna Berurah* concludes that where the *sakanah* is definite and the mode of help doubtful, then the one who is more zealous is praiseworthy (*se'if katan* 37). The implication is that when the action needed to alleviate the danger is definite and zeal is not a material issue, then perhaps either a Gentile or a minor should perform the act. In other words, where zeal could be a factor, then only an adult Jew should perform the act in question.

The *Aruch ha-Shulchan* disagrees with the Rama's position, citing two theories as to why the sages require that an adult Jew, and not a minor, should violate Shabbat in order to save someone in danger. The first is that it will counter the false assumption that an adult Jew may not violate Shabbat in order to help one in danger (Ran). The second is that a non-Jew or minor may not be as zealous as an adult (Tosafot, *Halacha* 6). Therefore, an adult Jew should be the one to act. Indeed, the *Aruch ha-Shulchan* concludes that in this particular halacha, when the phrase *gedolei Yisrael* is used, it means more than adult Jews. It refers to those who are *gedolim* – great in Torah. This teaches us that just as God instructed us to observe *Shabbat*, He commands us to violate it in order to save a person's life (*Orach Chayyim* 326:7).

The Eshel Avraham notes that common custom is to ask a Gentile, rather than a Jew, to violate Shabbat in order to save another Jew from danger. Though this custom goes against original sources, he suggests that it is logical because perhaps Shabbat may be violated only by a Jew when there is no doubt as to the danger. However, if the danger is doubtful rather than certain, then adult Jews should not violate Shabbat. Since most cases of danger are doubtful, the common custom has been to use the services of Gentiles or minors (see Eshel Avraham, *Mahadura Tanina*, 328). The uniqueness of this concept is the position that one reacts differently to a doubtful danger than to a clear one.

SAVING A DYING JEW ON SHABBAT (PART II)

Question: May one violate Shabbat in order to extend the life of a Jew whom physicians judge will not live beyond Shabbat itself? Although efforts to save this person will definitely extend his life, it is clear that even these measures will not enable him to live for more than a few hours. May one violate Shabbat for his sake nevertheless?

Response: Yes.

The *Mishna* rules: "Any danger to human life suspends [the laws of] the Sabbath" (*Yoma* 83a). Therefore, one must violate the Sabbath in order to save a human life. In seeking the rationale for this principle, the Talmud presents several explanations. One is as follows: "R. Shimon ben Menassia said, 'The children of Israel shall keep the Sabbath' [Exodus 31:16]. The Torah said: Profane one Sabbath so that the victim may keep many Sabbaths in the future" (*Yoma* 85b). The implication is that the quantity and quality of future observances outweighs the present violation of *Shabbat.*

What happens if physicians state that the person will not live to the next Shabbat? Indeed, the Biblical commentator Or ha-Chayyim (Exodus 31:16) contends that the concern is the issue of future observance. He notes that one may not violate Shabbat for the sake of a person who will not be able to observe future Sabbaths.

The rationale must be that the purpose of medicine is to heal. Thus, it may not be possible to extend life without healing, or at least improving the patient's future quality of life.

However, this position appears contrary to a well-established halachic precedent. The *Mishna* rules, "If debris fall on someone, and it is doubtful whether or not he is there, or whether he is alive or dead, or whether he is an Israelite or a heathen, one should open [even on the Sabbath] the heap of debris for his sake. If one finds him alive one should remove the debris, and if he be dead, one should leave him there [until the Sabbath is over]" (*Yoma* 83a, Soncino transaltion). On the phrase "if one finds him alive one should remove the debris," the Talmud comments, "But is that not self-evident?

164

No, the statement is necessary for the case that he has only a short while to live (*hayyei sha'ah*)" (*Yoma* 85a). This Talmudic principle is recorded in *Shulchan Aruch, Orach Chayyim* (329:3, 4). It is obvious that the Talmud does not suggest that the violation of Shabbat is dependent upon assurances of a minimum lifespan for the victim. Indeed, the matter is not discussed at all. There is not even a concern as to whether the victim will live beyond Shabbat itself. The Talmud merely rules that any effort to extend life, even for a short time, requires a violation of Shabbat. This definitely challenges the *Or ha-Chayyim*'s position.

The *Minchat Chinuch* cites the theory of the *Or ha-Chayyim*, ruling that it contravenes general halachic principles. The Talmud notes several reasons to explain the rules that suspend Shabbat in order to save a life. One such explanation was that such a violation ensured future observance. Yet the Talmud also reports the view of Samuel, who cites the verse, "He shall live by them" (Leviticus 18:5). From this he derives the rule, "He shall not die because of them" (*Yoma* 85b). Indeed, the Talmud rules that all theories except Samuel's may be refuted. Accordingly, violating Shabbat to save a person has nothing at all to do with concerns over future observance (*Melachot Shabbat* 39 – *Minchat Chinuch;* see also *Da'at Torah, Orach Chayyim* 329).

The *Mishna Berurah* fully discusses the parameters and implications of the rule that mandates violation of Shabbat in order to extend a person's life even for only a few hours. He rules that violation of Shabbat in such a case has nothing to do with the observance of future Sabbaths. In addition, he cites the commentary of the Meiri, who suggests that we must extend the person's life so that he will have time to repent of any sins that he may have committed. This, suggests the *Mishna Berurah,* may also lead to the misconception that some mitzvot are suspended because of the importance of observing other mitzvot in the future. This is simply not so. Mitzvot are suspended in order to save the life of the Jew *(chayyim shel Yisrael)*. For example, an infant certainly cannot repent sins, yet one is still required to violate Shabbat to save his or her life. Indeed, a person who suffers from a mental problem that impairs observance and repentance must also be saved. Even when the person is clearly dying (*gosses*), one must violate Shabbat in order to extend his or her life even for a short period of time. Therefore, concern as to whether a person will live to observe future Sabbaths should not hinder anyone from making every possible effort to save his life on Shabbat itself.

HOLDING THE HAVDALAH CUP

Question: During Havdalah on Saturday night, upon conclusion of the blessing over wine, should one continue to hold the wine goblet while chanting the other blessings?

Response: The *Shulchan Aruch* records the following proper procedure for the recitation of Havdalah: "The wine is held in the right [hand] and the myrtle in the left; [after] the blessing over the wine, one takes the myrtle in the right [hand] and the wine in the left; one recites a blessing over the myrtle and then returns the wine to the right [hand]" (*Orach Chayyim* 296:6).

This halacha is reported without any dissenting view. It delineates several important procedures: 1) Whenever one recites a blessing over a mitzvah upon an item that may be held, one should hold the item (wine, spices, *lulav*, and so on) in the right hand while reciting the blessing (see Taz, *Orach Chayyim* 296:6). 2) He should hold the second item to be used – in this case, the spices – in the left hand while reciting the first blessing. (3) When he recites the second blessing, he must still hold the wine in his left hand. The Mishna Berurah suggests that the rationale for not putting down the wine is that it is a mitzvah for all the blessings of Havdalah to be in some way related to the cup of wine (*Mishna Berurah* 296:31).

The *Aruch ha-Shulchan* remarks that it is not required to hold items in the left hand. His custom was not to hold the spice in the left hand while reciting the blessing over the wine. In addition, the wine was placed on the table while the blessing over the spices was recited. He concludes that it is a fine custom, though not obligatory, to hold the second item over which a blessing will be pronounced in the left hand while reciting the first (*Orach Chayyim* 296:17).

The Eshel Avraham reflected on his personal custom to hold the cup of wine in his right hand during Havdalah but not to hold any items in his left hand. Since he could not recall the rationale for not following the procedure detailed in the *Shulchan Aruch*, he suggested that any personal qualms (that lack substantiation) should not be sufficient grounds for discontinuing the

Shulchan Aruch's method. In addition, he notes that holding the items before and after the blessing may be a form of displaying affection and enhancement for the mitzvah (*chibbuv mitzvah*). Therefore, it is better to follow the *Shulchan Aruch*'s procedure (*Eshel Avraham, Mahadura Batra*, 296:6).

The concept of displaying affection for mitzvot is widespread. The Rama writes that the custom of kissing *tzitzit* and placing them over the eyes is a means of demonstrating love for the mitzvah (*Darchei Moshe, Orach Chayyim* 24). Therefore, the method set forth in the *Shulchan Aruch* should be the preferred one, with the recognition that after the fact it is only necessary to hold the item in one's hand while reciting the blessing over it.

For the correct procedure of a left-handed person, see the previous chapter "A Left-handed Person Holding the Kidush Goblet."

HAVDALAH OVER COFFEE

Question: May one recite Havdalah over coffee?

Response: This issue is a matter of dispute in rabbinic literature. Some authorities permit it while others do not. The basic concern is that Havdalah may be recited only over a beverage classified as *chamar medinah* – a national beverage. The debate hinges on the definition of this term.

The rationale to prohibit drinking coffee for *Havdalah* is as follows:

The Shaarei Teshuvah (*Orach Chayyim* 296) rules that milk may not be used for Havdalah.

The Minchat Ketanot (1:9) rules that beverages that have no alcoholic content are not considered *chamar medinah*.

Based upon the above, my grandfather, the Minchat Shabbat (96:9), felt that neither coffee nor milk should be used for Havdalah because neither contains alcohol.

Yet, in an addendum to the Minchat Shabbat (entitled *Mincha Chadashah*), my grandfather, Ha-Gaon Rav Shmuel Ha-Kohen, cites the *Kuntres Over Orah,* who noted that great Talmudic scholars indeed recited Havdalah over coffee or tea. On this basis, my grandfather suggests that perhaps *chamar medinah* represents any beverage served to guests. (Note: Before the publication of the *Mishna Berurah,* Russian, Galician, and Hasidic *rabbanim* used my grandfather's sefarim, the *Minchat Shabbat* and the *Ma'adanei Shmuel,* on the laws of Pesach, as basic authoritative guides for practical halacha.)

Interestingly, the ruling of the *Kuntres Over Orah* is also cited by the *Kuntres Aharon,* a commentary appended to the *Sefer Taamei ha-Minhagim* (365). It is noted that in the absence of wine (which is preferable for Havdalah), one may use sweetened tea or coffee. The *Kuntres Aharon* cites the *She'erit Yisrael,* who contends that since the era of the Baal Shem Tov, the custom has developed to use beverages made from honey for use during Havdalah as a symbol of sweetening life. He concludes by suggesting that this is an appropriate custom in our age.

Ha-Gaon Rav Sholom Mordechai ha-Kohen Schwadron (*Daat Torah, Orach Chayyim* 296) maintains that the reason that milk was forbidden for use in Havdalah was simply because it was not drunk as frequently then as it is today. In addition, he notes that milk should be permitted because it may induce a stupor comparable to the state induced by alcoholic beverages, for the Shach rules in the name of the Rambam that one who has drunk milk should not decide a matter of halacha (*Yoreh Deah* 242:20). The reasoning is that milk (probably hot milk) dims intellectual perception just as alcohol does. Yet he considers the issue a matter of doubt when it comes to a practical ruling.

In a discussion of whether a bride and bridegroom may eat before their wedding when the *chuppah* will not take place until late at night (several hours after *tzet ha-kochavim*), Ha-Gaon Rav Aryeh Levin made the following distinctions. On the day of the wedding the bride and bridegroom fast for two reasons: because the wedding day, on which their sins are forgiven, is comparable to Yom Kippur, and in order to avoid drinking intoxicating beverages that might cloud their awareness.

According to the first theory, once the day is officially over, so is the fast, even if the *chuppah* has not yet taken place. According to the second theory, the fast should continue until after the *chuppah*. The *Chochmat Adam* (129:2) rules that since this fast is not recorded in the Talmud, one may rely upon the first reason, and the young couple may break their fast at nightfall even though the *chuppah* has not yet taken place. However, he cautions that they should not drink intoxicating beverages. Ha-Gaon Rav Aryeh Levin (Rav of Raisha, Lithuania) notes that in such a case the couple should not drink milk because the Talmud states that one who drinks milk may not enter the Temple, since the prohibition on drinking milk before entering the sacred precincts is similar to that against drinking wine (*Bechorot* 45b). He also cites the Shach, who rules that one should not rule on halachic matters after drinking milk (*Yoreh Deah* 242:20). In addition, he cites many commentaries about Yael, who gave Sisera milk to drink because it induces an effect similar to that of intoxication (Judges 4). Therefore, the couple should avoid drinking milk (*Responsa Avnei Hefetz* 48).

Therefore, those who do not have wine, or who cannot drink wine, may rely upon halachic authorities for permission to drink coffee for Havdalah, providing it is sweet and contains milk.

SHOULD THE HAVDALAH CUP OVERFLOW?

Question: Should the cup that is used for Havdalah be filled to the point of overflowing?

Response: The Rama records an ancient custom of pouring some of the wine from the Havdalah cup onto the ground. His reason for this custom is that "any home where wine is not poured like water lacks a sign of a blessing" (see *Eruvin* 65a). According to the Rama, this custom takes place on Saturday night as a sign of a blessing for the coming week (*Orach Chayyim* 296:1).

The Magen Avraham rules that the custom of pouring wine onto the ground is not a halachic practice and should not be observed because it is a form of repudiating and disgracing the Havdalah blessing. He suggests that the proper custom is to fill the cup to the brim so that it can naturally overflow. Indeed, the Magen Abraham even contends that the custom that the Rama noted is an ex post facto reaction rather than a mandate for an *ab initio* procedure. Nowhere does it state that one should pour wine on the ground. Rather, it is written that if wine should be spilled, it is a *siman berachah*.

The Magen Avraham maintains that this custom was established so that people should not become angry if any wine was spilled. Since most are perturbed if wine spills, the custom was to note that such spillage is a good sign. Therefore, the halacha states that any house in which wine is spilled like water is a sign of blessing. Indeed, he notes that since pouring a great deal of wine over the brim constitutes a waste of food, the overflow should be small so as to prevent such waste (*Orach Chayyim* 296:11).

The Mishna Berurah cites the practice of creating a small amount of overflow so as not to cause waste (*Orach Chayyim* 206:5). My grandfather, the Minchat Shabbat, cites scholars who note that the common custom is not to pour or spill wine upon the ground but to make the cup overflow so that some will spill onto the table or into a saucer (*Minchat Shabbat* 96:19).

The *Aruch ha-Shulchan* modifies the Rama's position further, contending that even the Rama outlawed any deliberate pouring of wine on the ground or even on the table. Indeed, even to fill the cup up so much that wine overflows is wrong because it shows *bizui mitzvah* (contempt for the mitzvah). He suggests the following interpretation: the cup should be filled, like any cup that is used for a blessing (*Berachot* 57a). Yet one's hand may shake while one holds the wine cup and reciting the blessing. This natural hand movement causes some wine to spill from the cup. The halacha directs that if this takes place, one should not spill too much. Nevertheless, if a small amount spilled, the cup is still considered full. After Havdalah, we intentionally pour wine in a vessel to extinguish the lights, and some to place over our eyes (*Aruch ha-Shulchan* 296:11).

Based on the opinions cited above, it is obvious that the halachic authorities, first among them the Magen Avraham and the Mishna Berurah, opposed the spilling of wine and consider it wasteful.

Although the Rama noted the "custom of pouring out wine" to be specifically a procedure for Saturday night as a good sign for the coming week, some follow the same custom even for Friday night or Yom Tov *Kiddush*.

The *Mateh Moshe,* a compilation of customs by a disciple of the Maharshal, cites sources for the custom of pouring wine that indicate that it is limited to Saturday night. Some examples: "From Esau and Yishmael emanate seventy powers who are dormant on Shabbat but who, on Saturday night, seek to castigate Israel. The Hebrew word for wine is *yayin*, which has a numerical value of seventy. The wine (symbolizing the seventy troublemakers) is thrown to the ground right after Shabbat in order to weaken their powers." "At Havdalah we must formally separate ourselves from the children of Korach by pouring wine on the ground..." (*Mateh Moshe* 504. Such mystic (or kabbalistic) reasons simply do not apply on Shabbat or Yom Tov.

HAVDALAH: SYNAGOGUE AND HOME

Question: Is the Havdalah that is recited at home in any way different from that which is recited in the synagogue on Saturday night?

Response: The Rama cites a common custom to recite the verses that begin "Hinei El yeshuati" for a good omen before Havdalah in the home (*Orach Chayyim* 296:1). The obvious implication is that these introductory phrases are not included when Havdalah is recited in the synagogue. Therefore, the synagogues' Havdalah should commence with the blessing over wine. The Aruch ha-Shulchan suggests two reasons as to why the synagogue Havdalah does not include the introductory verses: 1) to teach the community that these phrases are only incidental, not essential to Havdalah, and 2) since the congregants already recited other verses (such as *Va-yiten lecha* in some congregations) for a good omen, no more are necessary (*Orach Chayyim* 296:8).

This rationale may also provide insight as to why on Friday night the synagogue Kiddush does not start with "Va-yechulu" but rather with the blessing itself. Two possible reasons are that there is no reason to repeat it since it was recited already, and that it may not be essential to Kiddush.

Many synagogues have the custom of reciting the entire Havdalah service, including the introductory phrases. I suggest that this custom may be based on the following. In his commentary on the Tur (*Darkei Moshe*), the Rama does not note that the introductory phrases of Havdalah should be recited only in the home. He merely states that they are not essential and are chanted for a "good sign." Perhaps the custom to make no distinction between reciting Havdala at home or at the synagogue is meant to symbolize that for Jews, there are never enough good omens. A petition for "good fortune" and a "good omen" is always in order, certainly also in the synagogue.

ABRAHAM AND SHABBAT

Question: Rabbinic scholars are not clear as to who was the first Jew/Hebrew. Some contend that Abraham had that status. Others believe that the status of being a Jew first took place at Mt. Sinai. Based upon the latter theory Abraham was not considered to be Jewish. This generates a major concern, for tradition has it that Abraham observed all the mitzvot prior to their being commanded at Sinai. Of concern is how Abraham related to Shabbat. If Abraham was classified as a Jew then he was obligated to observe Shabbat. In the event that Abraham is not regarded as the first Jew then it is problematic as to how he was permitted to observe Shabbat: for it is well known that a non Jew is not permitted to observe Shabbat. The question, therefore, is what procedure did Abraham follow to meet the obligations of such a conflicting status?

Response:

1. Abraham walked in a public thoroughfare while wearing tzitzit. As a Jew, he was observing the mitzvah of affixing fringes to his garment. Therefore, the fringes were not extraneous burdens, and wearing them did not violate Shabbat. However, if Abraham had been classified as a Gentile, then the tzitzit would have been considered an extraneous and unwarranted burden, and wearing them would have constituted a violation of Shabbat.

2. R. Pinchos Halevi Horowitz contends that the verse "Day and night shall not cease from working" (Genesis 8:22) means that the Gentiles reckon a calendar date change at sunrise. This means that for them, Saturday begins on Saturday morning at sunrise and continues until Sunday morning. However, Jews calculate a date change in the evening. Hence, for Jews, Shabbat lasts from Friday evening to Saturday evening. The prohibition against a Gentile observing Shabbat means that he may not rest on Saturday morning and continue such rest until Sunday morning. Thus the Patriarch Abraham may have satisfied his

uncertain status by doing work late on Saturday night. If he was classified as a Jew, of course, he observed Shabbat. If he was deemed a Gentile, then Shabbat, for him, ended on Sunday morning. Thus, by working late on Saturday night, he avoids being classified as a Shabbat observer (See *Panim Yafot,* Parashat Bereshit).

SIGNING ON SHABBAT TO BE ADMITTED TO A HOSPITAL

Question: A person is ill and needs to be hospitalized on Shabbat. However, he is not so ill that his life is considered to be in danger. At the admissions office, he is told that he must sign a form in order to be admitted. If the doctor or hospital staff should insist on refusing to admit him without a signature, may he sign the form on Shabbat?

Response: I have been in this situation myself. I dealt with it by explaining the religious prohibition against writing on Shabbat and giving my word to sign any necessary papers on Saturday night after Shabbat was over. This was usually effective. As more religious Jews frequent hospitals, the staff are aware that they do not write on Shabbat and generally do not insist that they sign forms on that day.

What of a case in which the staff sticks to the rules and absolutely refuses to admit a patient on Shabbat without a signature?

The following analysis is a summary of an Halachic decision by Ha-Rav ha-Gaon R. Tuvya Goldstein, Responsa *Emek Halacha* 1:14.

The *Mishna Berurah* (in the Be'ur Halacha commentary, 306:11) contends that the vast majority of halachic authorities maintain that writing two letters in Hebrew or any other language on Shabbat constitutes a Biblical violation of Shabbat. Therefore, it would appear that under no circumstances may a Jew sign his name on Shabbat unless he is deathly ill. The Rama rules that writing in languages other than Hebrew constitutes only a rabbinic violation (*Orach Chayyim* 306:11).

The Rama's position appears to be in direct opposition to an overt halacha in the Mishna. The Mishna of Tractate *Shabbat* (103a) states that writing two letters of any language is classified as a Biblical violation. Therefore, the Rama's decision seems to be contradicted by an undisputed Mishna.

To resolve this contradiction, the Noda bi-Yehuda, Ha-Gaon Rav Yechezkel Landau *z"l*, makes a fine distinction between a spoken language and the script in which it is written. It is well known that English words may be written in Hebrew, Arabic or Chinese script. On the other hand, Hebrew words may be transliterated – written using the English alphabet. Based upon this difference between a spoken and a written language, the Noda bi-Yehuda developed the ruling that any language written on Shabbat is deemed a Biblical sin as long as it was written in the [Hebrew] script of *ketav Ashurit*. If the writing is not done in *ketav Ashurit*, then the violation is only rabbinic (*Responsa Noda bi-Yehuda Tinyana, Orach Chayyim* 33) Thus, to write a name in English on Shabbat would only be a rabbinic violation.

Based upon the above position, Rav Goldstein ruled as follows. If a doctor asks a Jew to sign his or her name on Shabbat and there is no means of getting around this request, the Jew may do so. Why? The person is ill and it is a *she'at ha-dechak* – there is no way to get in the hospital without a signature. Therefore, in this situation one may rely on the Noda bi-Yehuda's position that one violates the Biblical laws of Shabbat only if one writes in *ketav Ashurit*, while writing on Shabbat in any other script constitutes a rabbinic violation. Rav Goldstein rules that the fact that a person is ill takes priority over the rabbinic prohibition against writing in any other script.

I suggest using a *shinui* as well. For example, right-handed Jews should sign with their left hands and vice versa. This is another way to avoid violating the injunction against writing.

PART V

FRONTIERS OF HALACHA

THE HALACHIC CONSIDERATIONS
OF A SHABBAT BUS

Introduction

IN AN ATTEMPT to enable Sabbath-observant Jews to use modern electrical conveniences on the Sabbath while still observing Jewish law, contemporary rabbinic scholars have displayed ingenuity in overcoming major halachic hurdles. The Shabbat elevator and the Shabbat (*gerama*) telephone are two prime examples of the modern use of Talmudic and halachic principles to make observant Jews' lives easier.

The philosopher Alfred North Whitehead once remarked that people in general are not overly concerned when science is faced with unanswerable questions. The fact that no proper response appears available at present does not faze the scientific community or the public at large. People have such strong faith in the validity of science that they are willing to consider all unanswerable questions as temporary ones that will eventually be answered. Therefore, people are unlikely to reject science as a whole because it is currently unable to provide an answer to a given question.

Yet when religious scholars are unable to respond to questions pertaining to basic beliefs or practices, the common reaction is to reject religious beliefs altogether. Whitehead suggests that our response to religion's inability to answer certain questions should be similar to our response to that of science. We should not be quick to discard our religious beliefs, and we should have faith that with enough time and research, religious scholars will develop proper, logical responses.

The fact that halachic scholars can now resolve modern issues in ways that would have been classified as overt violations of Jewish law in previous generations demonstrates the role of the passage of time in the halachic process. No longer operational is the old stringent standard articulated by Ha-Rav ha-Gaon R. Moshe Sofer, the author of the *Chatam Sofer* and the rabbi of Pressburg, Hungary that *"chadash asur min ha-Torah"* – innovation is prohibited. Based upon this principle, questions relating to the use of electric devices or other modern inventions on Shabbat were dismissed out of hand because such devices were new and unfamiliar.

This strict policy lends credence to the following commentary of Ha-Gaon ha-Rav Reb Chaim Shmuelovitz of blessed memory, the former Rosh ha-Yeshiva of the Jerusalem Mirrer Yershiva.

The Talmud records that the well-known scholar, Choni ha-Ma'agel, fell asleep for seventy years. Upon awakening, he returned to the *beit ha-midrash* and overheard the scholars there mourning his untimely death. "If only Choni were alive," they lamented, "he would be able to resolve all our halachic problems." But when Choni approached the rabbis and revealed his identity, they did not believe him. Dejected, he left (*Ta'anit* 23a).

Regarding this story, HaRav HaGoan Reb Chaim Shmuelovitz remarked, "What is a Torah sage? Is he not one who has mastered Torah knowledge?" Accordingly, Choni should have asked the local rabbis to pose halachic questions to him, since his responses would have proven his identity and status. Perhaps, Ha-Rav Chaim Shmuelovitz suggests, some halachic problems cannot be resolved by the sages of previous generations. Each scholar in each era must be attuned to the issues of his time and rule accordingly.

For this reason, *Pirke Avot* traces the chain of tradition. Moshe received the Torah from Sinai then transferred it to Yehoshua, Yehoshua to the Elders, the Elders to the Prophets, and the Prophets to the Men of the Great Assembly. No era relied completely on the previous generation for leadership, but had its own rabbi (*Sichot Mussar,* 5731, 19).

This suggests that an integral aspect of Torah tradition is that each generation's leaders have a unique opportunity to assess the halachic applicability of the inventions and circumstances of their time.

The Shabbat Bus: A Contemporary Concern

Century Village in West Palm Beach, Florida is a gated retirement community that contains approximately 6,800 residential units. To serve the residents, the village maintains several buses to transport them within the community's confines as well as to and from local shopping areas within West Palm Beach. The buses have a network of stops. Residents pay no fees for the rides and are not even required to show identification. While the drivers are all Gentiles, the passengers are a mixture of both Jews and Gentiles. The entire area of Century Village of West Palm Beach is enclosed with gates and an *eruv*. Directly outside is an Orthodox synagogue, Congregation Aitz Chaim, which is linked to the village by the eruv.

Question: May Jewish residents of Century Village ride the bus in order to attend the synagogue on Shabbat and return home afterwards?

Response: One issue of concern is whether Jews may derive benefit on Shabbat from actions forbidden to Jews yet performed by Gentiles on their behalf.

The *Shulchan Aruch* rules unequivocally that any action that a Jew is prohibited to do on Shabbat, he is precluded from requesting a Gentile to do on his behalf, even if the request is made prior to Shabbat (*Orach Chayyim* 307:2). The Rama adds that one may not even hint or suggest to a Gentile that he perform any action on a Jew's behalf on Shabbat (*ibid.*).

This prohibition, which is termed *amira le-akum,* is generally considered to be rabbinic in nature (*Shabbat* 150a). Though the Yere'im (113) rules that the prohibition is Biblical, Rav Yosef Engel contends that the Yerai'im limits the Biblical status to cases in which the prohibited action involves items owned by a Jew. However, in cases where a Jew asks a Gentile to perform an action for him with, for example, the Gentile's own fire, then even the Yerai'im would agree that it is deemed only a rabbinic prohibition (*Gilyonei ha-Shas,* Shabbat 150a).

Three major reasons are given for the prohibition.

Ve-daber davar. On Shabbat, a Jew should refrain not only from certain actions but also from speech that constitutes a violation of Shabbat (Rashi, *Avodah Zarah* 15a).

Shelichut. A Gentile who is asked to perform an action becomes the Jew's agent. Just as a Jew may not violate Shabbat, neither may his agent (Rashi, *Shabbat* 153a).

The sacredness of Shabbat. A Jew may not ask a Gentile to perform actions on Shabbat as a safeguard against Jews performing such actions themselves (Rambam, *Laws of Shabbat* 6:1).

The Avnei Nezer notes that according to the first reason, it would be permitted to make a request of a Gentile prior to Shabbat (Responsum of Avnei Nezer on *Orach Chayyim,* 43:6). Because of the other reasons, however, even this is prohibited.

It would appear that using the services of Gentiles on Shabbat to ride a Shabbat bus may be a direct violation of the principle of *amira le-akum*. However, it is necessary to assess whether this is halachically correct.

The Rama notes that some authorities maintain that *amira le-akum* is permissible for the performance of a mitzvah (Baal ha-Itur). Based on this concept, "many practiced the leniency of asking Gentiles to light candles for purposes of a [Shabbat] meal, [or] specifically for a wedding party or circumcision, and no one would protest [such practice]." However, the Rama concludes that since most halachic authorities dispute this premise, one should be stringent except in cases of great need (*Orach Chayyim* 276:2). Thus, the common custom was to use the services of Gentiles on Shabbat to perform mitzvot. Though the Rama disagrees with the basis for this practice, he notes that the contemporary religious authorities did not protest.

For several reasons, it is difficult to rely on this theory in modern times. The Magen Avraham notes that the reason for the lack of protest was the principle that it is better for Jews to sin unintentionally than to do so deliberately (*Orach Chayyim* 276:9). The implication is that even if those Jews were to be warned that the practice was forbidden, they would still continue to engage in it. Therefore, it is preferable that rabbis not tell them that it is wrong.

This cannot and should not be the guiding principle of pious Jews. Indeed, if Jews wish to hearken to the rabbis' decisions, the *Aruch ha-Shulchan* rules that one is required o protest the practice. The *Aruch ha-Shulchan* adds that the vast majority of authorities maintain that *amira la-akum* is prohibited for purposes of a mitzvah. In addition, he says, "In our day we have not heard [anyone] being lenient on this" (*Orach Chayyim* 276:14). Accordingly, this law cannot be the basis for its use.

Yet there are other ramifications and legal loopholes regarding *amira la-akum* that have pragmatic application. The *Mishna Berura* rules that on Friday it is permitted merely to hint or suggest to a Gentile that some service is required on Shabbat (*Orach Chayyim* 307:10). This means that only a formal, outright request on Friday, or a hint on Shabbat itself, to perform some action is prohibited.

Of interest is a case in which a Jew asks Gentile A to ask Gentile B to perform a task on behalf of a Jew. To the extent that the Jew never directly asked Gentile B to perform any task on Shabbat, this act may not be automatically prohibited. Indeed, the Ba'er Hetev (*Orach Chayyim* 307:3) cites a rabbinic debate on this issue. Rabbenu Gershon *(Avodat Gershuni)* prohibits the act, while the Chavat Yair contends that it is permissible (see Responsa Chavat Yair 49 and 53). The Shaarei Teshuva notes the leniency of the Chavat Yair and cites the Shevut Yaakov (vol. 3, 22), who agrees with this ruling (*Orach Chayyim* 321:6).

My grandfather, the Minchat Shabbat (90:25), and the Mishna Berura (307:24) rule that one may rely on the lenient view of the Chavat Yair when great loss is involved (*hefsed meruba*).

Though the Mishna Berura contends that whenever the lenient view is observed the Jew should not benefit personally from the *melacha* (307:24), the Pri Magedim disagrees and makes no such limitation. However, he contends that the second Gentile must not be aware that a Jew made the original request (*Mishbetzot Zahav* 276:5).

The Shmirat Shabbat Kehilchata suggests that one may perhaps rely on the Chavat Yair if the Gentile's act is for the purpose of a mitzvah (chap. 30, footnote 48). Yet the Minchat Shabbat warns that any questionable act, whether it is a mitzvah or not, may not be relied upon to offset *amira la-amira* (*Orach Chayyim* 90:29).

The Chatam Sofer rules that the debate concerning the propriety of asking one Gentile to ask a second Gentile to perform an action on Shabbat relates only to an instance where the Jew made his request to the first Gentile on Shabbat itself. In a case where the Jew requested Gentile A on Friday to ask Gentile B to perform an action on Shabbat, then all authorities permit it (Responsa, *Orach Chayyim* 60).

The Biur Halacha of the Mishna Berura cites this view of the Chatam Sofer, yet contends that it is a *chiddush* (an innovative theory) and is disputed by the Rashba (*Orach Chayyim* 307:2).

Based on the above citations, it would appear that the majority of halachic authorities would allow a Jew to ask a Gentile to perform a *melacha* on Shabbat on the following conditions: that the Jew *hint* on Friday to Gentile A to inform Gentile B of the need to perform an action on Shabbat. (The purpose is to attend synagogue services and to return to eat a Shabbat meal. This is a form of *safek sefeka*.)

According to the Baal ha-Itur, one may ask a Gentile, even on Shabbat, to facilitate the performance of a mitzvah, even to the majority who disagree.

Yet according to the Chavat Yair, one may ask Gentile A to tell Gentile B on Shabbat to perform an action, even to those who disagree.

Yet according to the Chatam Sofer, all authorities allow a Jew to ask Gentile A to inform Gentile B if he told Gentile A before Shabbat, even according to Mishna Berura, who implies that he disagrees.

Nevertheless, according to the Mishna Berura, one may hint to a Gentile on Friday to do a particular action on Shabbat.

According to the Shmirat Shabbat Kehilchata, one may rely on the Chavat Yair (and tell Gentile A even on Shabbat to tell Gentile B) in order to perform a *mitzvah*. Thus one certainly may rely on this process when the request was made on Friday (as per the Chatam Sofer), was merely in the form of a hint and its purpose was to perform a mitzvah.

A word of caution: in a recent conversation with a contemporary hasidic sage about the practical implementation (on other issues of Shabbat) of many of the principles discussed above (the theories of Chavat Yair and Chatam Sofer), the following objection was raised: The authorities cited above provide lenient rulings for using the services of a Gentile only when the need occurs infrequently. At such times, the *poskim* decreed that under certain limited guidelines, the action did not constitute a violation of Shabbat. However, this should not be construed as blanket permission to use such principles frequently in order to circumvent the prohibition of *amira la-akum*. Regular, weekly use of this leniency is prohibited because it is viewed as an effort to eliminate the prohibition altogether.

This novel and stringent approach does not necessarily match general procedures. The Rama (*Orach Chayyim* 276:2) noted that many people had the custom of asking Gentiles to light candles for Shabbat meals. Though the Rama and the majority of authorities objected to this practice for many halachic reasons, no reference is made to the issues of infrequent occurrence or regular usage. Accordingly, this distinction is a personal consideration that some may apply and others may reject with equally good reason.

According to the theories presented above, it appears that there are a variety of halachic ways to circumvent the prohibition of *amira la-akum*. Moreover, apart from the previous analysis, the best solution would be to set up a procedure wherein the Shabbat bus would make specific stops regardless of whether anyone got on or off. Thus, the non-Jewish driver would not be performing any specific action on Shabbat specifically for, or prohibited to, Jews. As long as non-Jewish passengers are on the bus, then no action is specifically performed for Jews.

Marit Ayin

Notwithstanding the halachic analysis discussed above, common sense dictates that Gentiles' actions on behalf of Jews should be forbidden in situations of *marit ayin*. In instances where *amira la-akum* does not apply, the act nevertheless may not be allowed if it leads others to believe, mistakenly, that a forbidden act is permitted. Moreover, when one may not perform a given act in public because of *marit ayin*, the prohibition applies even in the privacy of one's home.

Therefore, we must consider whether a Shabbat bus involves *marit ayin*. This appears to be a case where reasonable people could disagree.

Some might contend that *marit ayin* applies to this case because the non-observant public might presume it is permissible to ride buses on Shabbat exactly as one rides them during the week.

Indeed, many years ago Rabbi Sholom Klass, the publisher of *The Jewish Press* and a great halachic scholar, wrote, "It is forbidden to ride on a bus on Shabbat due to the prohibition of *marit ayin*. Others may see us riding the bus on Shabbat and, not knowing the details, would assume that it is permitted to drive your own car or ride in a vehicle driven by a Jew." He concludes, "It is absolutely forbidden to ride on any vehicle on Shabbat unless it is an emergency or a matter of life and death." (*Responsa of Modern Judaism,* Volume 3, 24, 25).

Others might suggest that Jews ride the Century Village Shabbat bus in a fashion that accords with halacha. A prime corroborating example is the use of *pareve* imitations of milk products during meat meals. The Rama explicitly rules that one may drink coconut milk together with meat, provided that some coconut shells are prominently displayed in order to show the source, so that there will be no concerns of *marit ayin* (*Yoreh Deah* 87:3). Indeed, when kosher non-dairy creamers first became popular, religious Jews prominently displayed the containers in order to prevent anyone from assuming that milk was being served at a meat meal. Since then, the use of non-dairy creamers has become so widespread that it is no longer common practice to display the containers at either private or public meals. People simply know that the cream at a kosher event at which meat is served is a non-dairy product. Should the same principle not apply to riding a Shabbat bus?

Perhaps it is necessary to display the Shabbat bus in a special way. Just as the use of the container solved the problem of *marit ayin* regarding margarine and non-dairy cream, perhaps the bus should carry a sign that reads: "This bus stops at all stations on the route" or even "This is a special Shabbat bus." The process should be comparable to that of the non-dairy creamers. Eventually it would become so familiar that even the sign might no longer be necessary.

Shabbat Violations Due to the Weight of the Passengers

Apart from the issues of *amira le-akum* and *marit ayin,* another halachic concern must be resolved – whether the weight of the passengers on the bus in any way contributes to an action that is prohibited on Shabbat. This issue was discussed by halachic scholars regarding the use of a Shabbat elevator.

Rabbi Yitzchok Weiss ruled that one may not ride a Shabbat elevator because the addition of one's body weight causes the elevator to work harder, thus drawing more current and increasing the use of electricity on Shabbat, which is forbidden (*Minchat Yitzchak* 3:60). This logic would apply to a Shabbat bus. As the number of passengers on the bus increased, the bus would carry more weight, thus requiring more fuel and current in order to operate.

However, not all halachic authorities accept this argument. Rav Yosef Eliyahu Henkin is cited as granting permission to ride in an automatic elevator because the passengers are passive, performing no action, while the mechanical elevator does the work (*Kol Kitvei ha-Gaon ha-Rav Henkin* 2:59).[1] Though Rav Henkin does not specifically discuss the issue of added weight, the fact that he granted general permission to ride in an automatic elevator implies that the question of violating Shabbat due to added weight is of no halachic concern to him. (See Rabbi Michael Broyde and Rabbi Howard Jachter, "The Use of Elevators and Escalators on Shabbat and Yom Tov," *The Journal of Halacha and Contemporary Society* 29 (Spring 1995): 62–88. These

---

[1] Acknowledgement and gratitude is extended to Rabbi Michael Broyde for clarifying the correct citation source: This teshuva actually appears on page 29 of *Teshuvot Ivra Responsa* 19(2) in *Kitvei Hagriya Henkin*, volume 2 (in the most current published edition).

rabbis cite the source for the Ha-Rav Henkin's ruling as *Kol Kitvei ha-Gaon Ha-Rav Henkin* 2:59.)[2]

Indeed, Rav Unterman, the former Chief Rabbi of Israel, discusses the issue of additional body weight in an elevator. His ruling is that this concern is not relevant and constitutes no violation of Shabbat. Rav Unterman's main argument is that there is already precedent to discount any concern for Shabbat violations due to increased weight of passengers. He notes that for generations countless Jews, including great Torah sages, traveled by ship. Throughout these voyages the ships sailed on Shabbat. No one ever contended that travel by ship was a violation of Shabbat because the passengers' body weight required the ship's engines to consume more fuel on Shabbat. He contends that this proves that any concern over Shabbat violations due to passengers' body weight is a non-issue. (Shevet Yehuda, p. 315) Rav Moshe Feinstein himself permitted the use of an elevator when there were no problems of *amira la-akum* (Iggrot Moshe, *Orach Chayyim* 2:80). The fact that Rav Feinstein does not even discuss the issue of added body weight shows that he deems it of no halachic concern.

The passengers on a bus are totally passive. They perform no action or active *melacha* at all. They are not even aware that they themselves, while passengers in a bus, are committing any act forbidden by Scripture. On Shabbat the key prohibition is the regard for an action prohibited on Shabbat, namely, *melechet machshevet* – the conscious realization that one is performing an act forbidden on Shabbat. The potential prohibition of added weight falls into the category of *lo ichpat lo* or *de-lo nicha lo,* or even a *mitasek* – that people either do not care about the effect, do not wish to receive any benefit, or are totally unaware of any prohibition. Where rabbinic prohibitions are at issue, many halachic scholars permit such situations. (See Rabbi Mordechai Willig, "Shabbat Laws related to Tractate Beitza." *Beit Yitzchok* 23:56, 77, and also Rabbi Michael Broyde and Rabbi Howard Jachter, *op. cit.*) Indeed, the Shulchan Aruch ha-Rav rules that a *pesik resha* performed by a Gentile is not a culpable action for a Jew, even it concerns a Biblical prohibition (*Orach Chayyim* 277:5; see also *Minchat Shabbat* 80:13).

---

[2] Ibid.

As such, the passengers are not performing any *melacha* on Shabbat. Under normal circumstances, the consensus ruling of the above scholars would be sufficient to proclaim that additional body weight is not a halachic concern. The contemporary problem is that Rabbi Levi Halpern, the director of the Institute for Science and Halacha, contends that while additional body weight does not affect an elevator's operation when it rises, the passengers' body weight enables the elevator to descend more quickly. Thus, the passengers' body weight provides a benefit – an added factor which, says Rabbi Halpern, should be forbidden on Shabbat (See *Maaliot ba-Shabbat,* Chapters 6 and 13).

The *Shmirat Shabbat ke-Hilchata* (Vol. 1, 23:49) notes Rav Halpern's position but rules that great halachic scholars permit the use of these elevators for descent as well. In a footnote to this ruling, he cites Rav Shlomo Zalman Auerbach *z"l* as the source of the lenient position. Rav Auerbach's argument is that *melechet machshevet* is forbidden on Shabbat. In an elevator, the passengers perceive no change in its rate due to their body weight. "Everything takes place exactly as it would have without the presence of the passengers." Their riding in the elevator therefore constitutes an ineffectual action. Rav Yisrael Rosen, the director of the Zomet Institute, interprets Rav Auerbach's statements to mean that since a deliberate action must take place on Shabbat, then an ineffectual action cannot be considered deliberate for halachic purposes. (See Rav Yisrael Rosen, "The Shabbat Elevator." In *Crossroads – Halacha and the Modern World,* vol. 1, 260.)

Indeed, Rav Rosen discusses all aspects of probable Shabbat violations due to the passengers' body weight. He concludes the following:

On Shabbat, the passengers' body weight is not considered responsible for any culpable action.

Even if weight is an action, this is only if it acts alone. If another force is using one's weight, the weight is only a tool in the hands of the other, and not an agent. The motor is the sole agent and not the man, who is being moved by the motor.

Even should one assume that weight is an action and the man an agent, one may be lenient for it would be in the category of "an accessory is not accountable," even though it is a case of a partnership between a man and an outside force.

"The last point is sufficient to permit use of an elevator where there are only rabbinic prohibitions involved. The first two points are suffcient to permit even Torah prohibitions" (Rav Rosen, *Crossroads*, 273).

It is significant that Rabbi Halpern's new and innovative assessment of the technical aspects of descending elevators is not relevant to the issue of the Shabbat bus. The passengers' body weight does not improve the bus's operation, especially in this case, where the terrain of Century Village, Florida is flat. Therefore, the Shabbat bus is in reality a "horizontal elevator" and may be halachically permitted.

A system may be set up whereby the bus stops at specific areas on Shabbat regardless of whether there are passengers on board. This would eliminate the concerns for *amira le-akum*. In addition, proper signs may distinguish the Shabbat bus from other types of vehicles in order to solve the problem of *marit ayin*. Just as coconut shells mark the usage of coconut milk as unique and different, the signs indicate that this bus is different from the others.

Uvda de-Chol

To the extent that the Shabbat bus may appear to some to be a form of *uvda de-chol*, a weekday activity and not a Shabbat endeavor (Rabbi Klass, *op. cit.*, also used this concept to forbid riding a bus on Shabbat) perhaps as a form of halachic policy, the original halachic permission should be restricted to the elderly or infirm who cannot attend the synagogue on Shabbat without such assistance. In other words, the general policy would be to withhold blanket permission to ride a Shabbat bus. Since this is an accommodation for those who feel that riding such a bus violates the spirit of Shabbat if not the letter, it certainly may be used by those who are ill, infirm or suffer from weakness due to age. Indeed, halacha regularly makes many exceptions for the ill and the infirm.

Some rabbis contend as a general guideline that it is best not to rely routinely on lenient positions (see Rabbi Broyde and Rabbi Jachter, *op. cit.*, 88). *Shmirat Shabbat ke-Hilchata* (23:50–51 and 30:54) is cited as advising Jews not to live in certain high-rise buildings that use two lenient positions each Shabbat: to rely on the services of a Gentile dorman and to descend in an elevator. These leniencies do not apply to the Shabbat bus, which will stop at every station regardless of whether anyone needs to get on or off there, thus solving the problem of *amira la-akum* regarding asking or causing the bus driver to stop for pickup or drop off. Also, unlike the case of the descending elevator, the passengers' body weight will generally have no effect on the bus, especially in a flat area. As long as permission to ride a Shabbat bus is granted only to the old, ill and infirm who cannot attend synagogue without it, there is no good reason to withhold permission simply because some people prefer to be more stringent.

Addendum

The above teshuva was sent to a number of rabbonim for review and comment. Since the issues involved are controversial, it was not surprising that very few responded. Some rabbis, however, informed me verbally that they felt it prudent not to publish any analysis on this issue for fear of people on the extreme right, who engage in vicious personal attacks against those who support a more lenient view. In other words, the merit of the positions articulated above would not be granted a fair hearing or even considered. One hopes that such fears are not grounded in reality.

The response of Rav Moshe Tendler was that the Shabbat bus is categorically prohibited (see Appendix A). His main argument was that since the passengers' body weight would increase the amount of fuel and electricity that the bus used, each additional passenger would be responsible, to some extent, for forbidden use of electricity on Shabbat.

What is surprising is that Rav Tendler disregarded the positions of the Gedolim, who ruled that additional body weight causes no violation of Shabbat. Indeed, Rav Unterman, the former Chief Rabbi of Israel, formally ruled that additional body weight is in no way responsible for a violation of Shabbat. He based his ruling on the example of ship travel noted above. Rav Tendler neither mentions this ruling nor attempts to refute it.

However, in a general dismissive statement, he notes, "Those poskim who do not relate to the 'added weight' concern were unaware of the fact that added weight calls forth more electromotive force." While it is well known that Rav Tendler is not only a Gaon in Torah but also a distinguished scientist, it is difficult to presume that Rav Unterman, the former Chief Rabbi of Israel, and all the other poskim were unaware of the idea that additional weight generates more usage of electric power. As stated above, although Rav Unterman was aware of it, he ruled that it constitutes no violation. Finally, while Rav Tendler's fear that a halachic leniency regarding a Shabbat bus may be extended to other issues is understandable, the fact that it is limited to a single gated community would seem to obviate this problem.

Indeed, further research shows that Rav Unterman was not the only halachic decisor who ruled that an increase in the number of passengers does not automatically constitute a violation of Shabbat.

Rav Shilo Raphael, the former Av Beit Din of the Rabbinical Court in Jerusalem, once corresponded with the Tzitz Eliezer on the following issue. Could a man who had not yet accepted the sanctity of Shabbat on Friday afternoon be allowed to drive his wife to and from the Western Wall after she had lit the Shabbat candles? The Tzitz Eliezer answered that he could not. The prohibition was based on the ruling of the Chatam Sofer (Responsa 97), who contended that on Shabbat, one was not permitted to ride on a train driven by a Gentile even when most of its passengers were not Jewish. The rationale was that the Jewish person's body was not at rest. This was considered a violation of the Ramban's position that on Shabbat it is a mitzvah to rest (see Parashat Emor). In addition, train travel was deemed not as restful as travel by ship. For this reason, the rabbis permitted the latter even on Shabbat. Therefore, one was not permitted to ride in a car on Shabbat because the body would not be at rest. (See *Responsa Tzitz Eliezer*, Section 11, paragraphs 21–22.)

Rav Raphael disputed the basis for this prohibition. His argument was that according to the Ramban, a violation of the mitzvah to rest occurred only in a case where someone performed actual physical labor throughout Shabbat. One should not consider sitting in a seat comparable to working on Shabbat.

In addition, the sea is not smooth at all times. During storms or rough weather, the movements of the ship on the waves would make the ride extremely uncomfortable. Apart from the logical rejection of the allusion to the Ramban, Rav Raphael located a responsum by Rav Zvi Pesach Frank, former Chief Rabbi of Jerusalem (*Har Tzvi* 293) in which he does not even consider the possibility of prohibiting the case because one's body is supposedly not at rest during car travel.

Rav Frank's case relates directly to the issue at hand. On a Yom Tov that followed Shabbat, he permitted members of a Chevra Kaddisha to travel to a cemetery in a van driven by a Gentile driver. The halachic issue was whether the driver was generating more fire in the car's engine (*hav'ara*) because of the large number of passengers. Rav Frank ruled that the increased use of fuel was not due to the number of passengers but rather to the driver's wish to travel more quickly or to maintain a certain speed. The passengers were not concerned about the speed at all. Therefore, according to Rav Frank's ruling, the increased use of fuel is an issue only for the Gentile driver and has no halachic bearing upon the Jewish passengers.

Based upon Rav Frank's ruling, Rav Raphael made the following decision. A young girl who had been injured on a Friday night had to go to the hospital for tests. After the tests were completed, she was told that she did not need to stay in the hospital and could go home if she wished. Two halachic questions emerged: could she be driven home by a non-Jewish driver, and could her father accompany her in the car even though it was Shabbat?

Rav Raphael ruled as follows: A young child is considered a *choleh she-ein bo sakkanah* (a sick person whose life is not in danger; see *Orach Chayyim* 276:1, Rama). Indeed, the Rama rules that for this reason, one may ask a non-Jew to prepare food for a child who has nothing to eat (327:16). In other words, one may ask a non-Jew to violate even a Biblical mitzvah in order to care for a child. Because the little girl was frightened of remaining in the hospital, it was definitely permissible to have a non-Jew drive her home on Shabbat.

Now the question arose as to whether her father was permitted to accompany her in the car. Based on Rav Frank's ruling that passengers who merely sit in a car driven by a Gentile do not violate Shabbat, Rav Raphael ruled that he was permitted to ride together with his daughter (*Mishkan Shilo*, 133–135).

Of special interest is the letter from Rabbi Norman Lamm, former President of Yeshiva University (see appendix B). He notes that while visiting India he was given a memento, a ticket for a Shabbat bus. Years ago, special tickets were issued to the Jewish community in order to enable them to ride a bus to the synagogue on Shabbat. Indeed, I have heard stories of such occurrences from various sources. My assumption was that at one time, a Sefardi rav may have permitted congregants to use a bus on Shabbat. Though we do not know who he was or the circumstances of the case, the popular stories, together with the actual Shabbat tickets, give the impression that this was an accepted fact of life in that community. Incidentally, I do not believe that Rabbi Lamm's concern over the issue of *techum Shabbat* is relevant to a Shabbat bus that operates within a gated community.

The most extensive response came from Rav Yosef Carmel, dean of the Eretz Hemdah Institute in Israel, which ordains rabbis and rabbinic judges. It also publishes halachic responses to questions from communities throughout the world in a responsa series entitled *Be-mareh ha-bazak*. Apart from noting several typographical errors that are corrected in the text, Rav Carmel directs readers' attention to two articles published in the third volume of *Be-mareh ha-bazak* that were personally approved by the noted halachic decisor who was also the founding leader of the Institute, Rav Shaul Yisraeili *z"l*.

In Responsum 38, a community in Cali, Colombia asked whether a Gentile could drive an elderly and infirm man to and from the synagogue on Shabbat. The decision was that if there was any other way for him to attend the synagogue without violating any laws of Shabbat, he would be forbidden to ride in a vehicle driven by a Gentile. However, if the only way that he could attend synagogue was if a Gentile drove him there, then he could rely upon the ruling of the Baal ha-Itur, who permits violating a rabbinic ordinance in order to perform a mitzvah.

This permission enabled an elderly Jew to retain a relationship with his synagogue even after he had lost the ability to walk. However, the leniency could not be used every week. The rationale is that the lenient ruling should not be deemed permanent but used only occasionally (see note 2 of the responsum). In Responsum 37, it was noted that permission was granted not only for one Jew but rather for many Jews to be driven to synagogue and back on Shabbat. Indeed, it was noted that hospitals in Jerusalem customarily use a bus to bring doctors and nurses home on Shabbat (per n. 12).

What is fascinating is that at no time is there any mention of a Shabbat violation due to increased use of electricity due to the amount and weight of passengers in the vehicle. The entire concern is simply the violation of *amira la-akum*. As was pointed out previously this violation could be muted by a *remez* (hint) together with an *amira la-amira* before Shabbat.

Rav Carmel maintained that a Shabbat bus is permissible under the following conditions:

That the doors open manually.

That the bus is labeled clearly as a Shabbat bus.

That only non-Jewish drivers are employed.

That it is stressed that the matter is a *she'at ha-dechak* and that the bus is permitted only every other week.

That the local community view the decision as a means of aiding the enjoyment and Shabbat observance of its members and not as a creeping violation of Shabbat itself.

Conclusion

It is clear that halachic opinions differ regarding the permissibility of a Shabbat bus. The negative view is that its use involves possible Biblical and rabbinic violations. In addition, opponents of the bus fear that its use may lead to additional violations of Shabbat. Nevertheless, some distinguished halachic scholars disagree. Indeed, we should not question or dismiss the halachic acumen, piety and concern for Jewish communal life of those who rule leniently.

The following halachic ruling may suggest a compromise position.

It is well known that there is no scriptural prohibition against carrying on Shabbat in the street concerning a child who can walk by himself (the principle of *chai nosei et atzmo*). In addition, the majority of halachic scholars maintain that our contemporary streets do not contain a thoroughfare by scriptural standards (in other words, they are not a *reshut ha-rabbim de-oraita*). Our streets are deemed a *carmolit,* which means that carrying therein is prohibited only from a rabbinic viewpoint. Accordingly, carrying a child in the streets is prohibited only if we combine both rabbinic bans. Interestingly, the Pri Megadim rules that in such a case it is permissible for the sake of a mitzvah (*Mishbetzot Zahav, Orach Chayyim* 325:1). My grandfather, the renowned posek, the Minchat Shabbat, notes that alleviating the pain or anguish (*tza'ar*) of a child is tantamount to performing a mitzvah. This concept, together with the Pri Megadim's ruling, is the halachic source that allowed Jews in Europe to carry their small children outdoors even in areas that had no eruv. Though the Minchat Shabbat notes that many great sages, including the Magen Avraham (308:71) and the Shulchan Aruch ha-Rav

(308:81), disagree with the Pri Megadim's ruling, one should not reprimand those parents who rely on it. The Minchat Shabbat concludes that this legal lenient position should not be adopted as a ruling *le-chat'hila* but merely as a reason not to criticize those who do carry children in areas that have no eruv (*Minchat Shabbat* 82:28).

So too with the Shabbat bus. Perhaps it should not be used *le-chat'hila*. Nevertheless, we should be tolerant of those elderly, infirm Jews who wish to rely upon the more lenient position – in other words, neither *heter* nor criticism. My own feeling here is: *Asher lo ya'aseh ha-sechel, ya'aseh ha-zeman.*

APPENDIX A

Kevod ha-Rav ha-Gaon R. Yaakov Simcha Cohen Shlita,

Sooner or later I answer all correspondence. With the academic year ended at RIETS I am taking the mail I triaged for later.

Ya'asher kochecha for the "Shabbat Bus tentative responsum." I made the following notes while studying it that impact on the potential pesak.

Those *poskim* who do not relate to the "added weight concern" were unaware of the fact that added weight calls forth more electromotive force.

A person's weight is tantamount to ma'aseh be-yadayim – as defined in halachos of "Five she-yashvu al ha-safsal." Those who wrote otherwise are "to'im bi-devar Mishna."

Le-maskana – the heter would destroy the sanctity of the Shabbos. It would be extended to other "good deeds" like visiting parents, hospital patients, attending rallies and even earning money on Shabbos to pay yeshiva tuition.

As the Ramban concluded in his Derasha le-Rosh ha-Shana, the *aseh* of "Shabbaton" prohibits any activity that debases the sanctity of the Shabbos.

Be-virchat kol tuv,
(Ha-Rav) Moshe Dovid Tendler
[2005]

APPENDIX B

From: Rabbi Dr. Norman Lamm
To: Rabbi J. Simcha Cohen

Dear Rabbi Cohen:

Your paper, which you were kind enough to send me for review and comment, is quite interesting. You seem to have covered all the relevant sources, both pro and con, under the rubric of *amirah le-akum, marit ayin,* increased weight, and *uvda de-chol.*

Just two comments, one historical and the other halakhic.

When I visited India, especially the Bene Israel in Bombay and environs, I heard of a system that had been in use but discontinued a few years before my arrival there in 1961. The practice was for Jews to purchase special "Shabbat coupons" in advance, and to be presented to the conductor or driver of the bus on Shabbat. At home (I am writing this from Florida) I have a One Anna Shabbat coupon given to me as a souvenir. I do not know on whose authority this was done, but I presume there was a *she'elah* asked and a *teshuvah le-heter* obtained. Of course, considering the lack of erudition amongst this sector of world Jewry, that does not qualify as adequate precedent, but it surely may be worth mentioning.

Second, my halakhic point. Granted your four items mentioned above, you omitted what may be the most important and probably the most difficult and resistant – the question of *techumin.* There are many authoritative views on most issues under this heading, and it requires great *yishuv ha-daat.* Instead of presenting it all here, in an email, I refer you to Rabbi Eliezer Waldenburg's *Tzitz Eliezer,* Part I, No. 21.

My personal feeling is that even if you should be able to marshal support for the use of such a vehicle on Shabbat, and if you can overcome the objections raised by Rabbi Waldenburg referred to above, you ultimately must wrestle with the fact that in the anticipated use of this vehicle on Shabbat, there always exists the danger that it will travel *chutz le-techum.* If the discussion centered upon a train or a trolley car, both of which are tethered to tracks that operate only within the city limits, one might investigate the possibilities of permissiveness even further. However, if you are speaking about a bus, which is free to roam wherever the driver takes it, you will not be able to overcome the prohibition of travel beyond the *techum*.

I hope this proves at least somewhat helpful. Good luck, and do keep me informed as to developments.

[2005]

APPENDIX C

Your discussion of the "Shabbat buses" issues was detailed and quite interesting. We hope that our comments will be helpful.

First, minor technical corrections:

On the third page, you quote ("Though the *Mishna Berurah*...") a *machlokes* between the *Mishna Berurah* (307:11) and the *Pri Megadim* (M.Z. 276:5). The *Pri Megadim* (M.Z. 307:2) actually agrees with the *Mishna Berurah* (307:11).

On the next page you cite ("This novel...") the Rema (307:2) regarding Gentiles lighting candles for Shabbat meals. We assume you meant the Rema (276:2).

On the following page you quote Rav Henkin from *Kol kitvei ha-Gaon ha-Rav Henkin* 2:59 (as do Rabbi Broyde and Rabbi Jachter in their article). We are familiar with Ezrat Torah's 2 volume *Kitvei Ha-Rav Henkin,* but were unable to find it there. Is *Kol kitvei* etc. a different publication?[1]

Now some comments regarding the content of the discussion:

Regarding the above mentioned disagreement between the *Mishna Berurah* (307:24) and the *Pri Megadim* (M.Z. 276:5) it would appear to us that the *Mishna Berurah* does not argue; the *issur hana'ah be-diavad* of the *Mishna Berurah* should only apply when the second Gentile realizes that he is acting on behalf of a Jew. The Pri Megadim, on the other hand, rules leniently only in the case when the second Gentile believes he is acting on behalf of another gentile. In our case, the bus driver sees who is boarding his bus, and thus has (also) Jews in mind while driving.

Regarding the bus making specific stops regardless of whether anyone entered or exited, would the driver also open the doors independently? Would the bus be such that opening and closing the doors involve a Shabbat

---

[1] Acknowledgement and gratitude is extended to Rabbi Michael Broyde for clarifying the correct citation source: This teshuva actually appears on page 29 of *Teshuvot Ivra Responsa* 19(2) in *Kitvei Hagriya Henkin*, volume 2 (in the most current published edition).

prohibition? (Even if so, one can still be lenient if the driver is able to open it manually without Shabbat violation, as in *Mishna Berurah* 276:31).

Representing Eretz Hemdah, we would be amiss not to reference the response published in *Be-mareh ha-baẓak* III:37–38 (authored by *avrechim* in the *kollel*, and authorized by Rav Shaul Yisraeli, *ẓt"l*). Siman 37 hesitatingly suggests having a non-Jew pick up and drop off Jews coming to *shul*, but the discussion is for a very large *she'at ha-dechak*. Siman 38 allows reliance on the Ba'al ha-Itur in a *she'at ha-dechak*, but only every few weeks (so as to only be occasional, as you yourself quote in the name of "a contemporary Hasidic sage"). Both of these responsa refer to a non-Jew driving Jews only, which admittedly is worse than our case, in which Jews and non-Jews would presumably ride on the bus together.

Volume V:34, which was written after the passing of Rav Yisraeli, *ẓt"l*, notes that it is clearly preferable for congregants to ride on a metro train than to drive themselves to shul, and that it may be appropriate for the Rabbi to suggest the train as a better means of transportation. Here to, however, caution is emphasized, due to the feared "slippery slope" which you yourself note.

Our personal inclination is that if the bus is clearly labeled as a "Shabbat bus," is announced as appropriate only for those too weak to walk on their own, and even then only to be used for transportation to and from *shul*, it could be positive, provided that someone familiar with the community feels it would be necessary. (One must, of course, verify that only non-Jewish drivers are used). However, we would recommend monitoring public impression (not only before implementation but also after) so as to gauge whether people view this as either a religious farce or a sweeping abrogation of hilchot Shabbat (in which case the service should be discontinued).

We would also like to suggest the aforementioned ruling of Rav Yisraeli, *ẓt"l* (*Be-mareh ha-baẓak* III:38) of having the Shabbat bus run only occasionally (or perhaps alternate weeks, etc.) so as to stress that we are dealing with a *she'at ha-dechak*.

B'hatzlacha,
Rabbi Yosef Carmel
In the name of Eretz Hemdah Rabbis
[2005]

POSTSCRIPT

I⊤ HAS COME to my attention that in New York City as well as in downtown West Palm Beach a new form of public transportation has emerged: namely, a rickshaw attached to a bicycle. It is based upon the Asian concept of the rickshaw. However, instead of a person running while holding the rickshaw, a bicycle is attached to the rickshaw and the driver rides the bicycle.

This form of transportation certainly has positive ramifications for Shabbat. As mentioned in "A Tricycle on Shabbat" above, the Debritziner Rav, Rav Moshe Stern, ruled that a young child may ride a tricycle on Shabbat. Bicycles are prohibited on Shabbat for two reasons: they may break down and one would violate the Shabbat by repairing them, and riding them is a form of *uvda de-chol,* not a Shabbat activity (*Responsa Be'er Moshe,* VI:16).

One may ask why there is no prohibition against using a tricycle on Shabbat simply because it is not a Shabbat activity. The most logical answer is that since we are not concerned that a child will repair a broken tricycle, the secondary concern for *uvda de-chol* by itself is not an issue. Accordingly, a rickshaw bicycle driven by a non-Jew would also not be prohibited because of the concern that he might repair the bicycle on Shabbat, since a Gentile may repair anything he wishes on Shabbat. The prohibition of repair applies only to Jews, not to Gentiles. Using all of the methods mentioned above, one could arrange, well within the bounds of Halacha, for a bicycle rickshaw to transport Jews who are unable to walk to and from the synagogue on Shabbat. This would involve no Biblical violations at all.

ABOUT THE AUTHOR

THE SCION OF eighteen generations of rabbis, Rabbi J. Simcha Cohen is the author of six highly regarded books of Halacha. He was ordained by HaRav R. Yitzchok Hutner *z"l*, of Yeshivat Rav Chaim Berlin, and has served as community Rabbi in New Jersey, California, and Australia. Rabbi Cohen is the founder of a national rabbinic think tank and served at the helm of several national and local rabbinic and communal organizations. He is the recipient of the Rabbinic Leadership Award from the West Coast Region of the Orthodox Union and was honored with the "Jerusalem Prize" in 2002 for Rabbinic Leadership and Scholarship. His column, *Halachic Questions*, appears in *The Jewish Press*. His writings have been acclaimed as "remarkable achievements" that "succeed in creating genuine Torah excitement" and include *How Does Jewish Law Work* (vol. 1 and 2), *Timely Jewish Questions: Timeless Rabbinic Answers, Intermarriage and Conversion, The Jewish Heart*, and *The 613th Commandment*. Rabbi Cohen lives with his wife Shoshana in West Palm Beach, Florida, where he is the spiritual leader of Congregation Aitz Chaim.